GOD
IN THE MOMENT

GOD
IN THE MOMENT

Making Every Day a Prayer

KATHY COFFEY

 Loyola Press

Chicago

 Loyola Press

3441 North Ashland Avenue
Chicago, Illinois 60657

Interior design by Kathy Kikkert

Library of Congress Cataloging-in-Publication Data

Coffey, Kathy.
   God in the moment : making every day a prayer / Kathy Coffey.
      p.   cm.
   Includes bibliographical references.
   ISBN 0-8294-1174-7
   1. Prayer—Catholic Church.   I. Title.
BV210.2.C585 1999
248.3'2—dc21   98-52474
                                                               CIP

Printed in the United States
99 00 01 02 03 / 10 9 8 7 6 5 4 3 2 1

FOR MY DAD

Joseph Rogers

whose ways are kind
whose language is graceful
whose prayer is poetic

CONTENTS

FOREWORD

You are going to like this book and its author. After all, you
would not have it in your hands if you were not attracted to
God and desirous of developing your relationship with God. I
believe you will be glad you picked it up. Not only does Kathy
Coffey talk the talk, but she walks the walk. She demonstrates
in this book that she acts on her faith that God is ingredient in
this world, working at every moment to get our attention and
to draw us into a relationship of friendship and intimacy.

God—Father, Son, and Holy Spirit—desires this universe
into existence in order to invite us into the intimate life of the
Trinity. The early Christian theologians who spoke Greek
coined a wonderful phrase to describe the inner life of the
Trinity: *perichoeresis, peri-* meaning "around" and *choeresis* meaning
"dancing"; hence, "dancing around." Our word "choir" derives
from *choeresis*. So we need to think of music and dance and
words together as a symbol of the inner life of God.

With creation, and especially with the incarnation of the
Word of God, this dance becomes the ground of our universe.
One Person of the Trinity is flesh of our flesh, bone of our
bone, tied to the whole creation bodily. The dance of the
Trinity in some mysterious way pervades the universe.

At every moment of existence we are surrounded by this
perfect dance. At every moment of existence we are being
drawn by the music of this eternal dance to become conscious
participants in it. God wants us to be partners in the dance, to
be so intimate that we share the inner life of the Trinity. Kathy

Coffey seems to live out of this conviction. Her book aims to help people like herself, people with jobs and families and commitments, who have become aware of the music of the dance and desire to develop their ability to live more consciously in its rhythms.

In this book you will meet someone like yourself who wants to be in conscious contact with God; to pray, that is, as often as possible in a day packed with chores, work, family obligations, frustrations, and joys. Kathy Coffey writes in a conversational style and uses anecdotes from her own life. The book invites conversation with her. She makes suggestions for reflection and prayer after each chapter, suggestions that could lead to fruitful dialogues with her in imagination, if not by letter. More than anything else, in this book you will meet a woman who is herself in love with God and the dance of God, who has learned, through prayer and reading, ways to let God into her life, and who has the talent of writing so that she can share her hard-won wisdom with us, her readers. Enjoy.

WILLIAM A. BARRY, S.J.

1

MANY FACES

Toward a Broader

Definition of Prayer

God works in moments.

—OLD FRENCH SAYING

Oh, God!" we yelp as it becomes crystal clear that the truck barreling down on us intends to run the yellow light. "Help!" we moan as we spot the return address of an IRS audit team in our pile of mail. "Oh, Jesus," we breathe when we can read the grim diagnosis on the doctor's face even before she speaks.

For many people, these agonized cries in the face of disaster constitute prayer. Crisis prompts their only communication with the Deity. Their prayers are heartfelt, urgent, direct— though some might argue that this approach to prayer is like phoning a friend only when we desperately need a favor.

Most of us feel less guilty about making that call if we've already established a context for it. If we have wasted time with the friend, know her quirky habits, share lots of meals, run a few of *her* stupid errands, and frequently get lost on the highway together, we're less reluctant to plead, "My basement is flooding! Can you bring your Shop-Vac right away?"

God, like a friend, doesn't rule out last-ditch pleas. But it's nice, when we suddenly find ourselves in a predicament, if our yelps of pain, surprise, or grief are set in the context of an ongoing relationship. We aren't afraid to contact heaven suddenly when we've established an ongoing conversation, when we're always trying to deepen our relationship with God. We can approach God confidently, because we've learned to have an attitude of prayer in all circumstances.

PEOPLE AT PRAYER

Such an attitude is possible for all of us. Unfortunately, what may hamper this attitude for some is a stereotyped notion of prayer. People may get stuck on one face of prayer: to them, it's an easily recognizable activity. The folks kneeling in church, fingering rosary beads—surely *they* are praying. The monks or nuns in brown robes, singing the Psalms as they have for centuries—we *know* they are praying.

Yet if we are too certain that only saying formal words with other people constitutes prayer, we may be closing ourselves to other possibilities. Outworn ideas of prayer can get stuck in a narrow niche, growing mossy and irrelevant. If we rethink prayer in broader terms, we are not being irreverent. Rather, knowing how much we need prayer, we seek to make it vital, attractive, and accessible.

Prayer can in fact wear many faces. Some may startle; some may simply surprise. Nor is there always correspondence between the outer face and the inner motive.

A nurse at work, for instance, might be deeply involved with patients and paperwork. But sometimes she pauses to consider that she works not only for the paycheck that supports her children. She recalls also that her work taps God's unique gifts to her; her compassion contributes to healing the suffering Christ in human beings. That pause to reflect may last only the length of a coffee break, but it transforms her work. She is centered and reenergized by knowing that God goes with her, into the oncology ward as well as into the coffee shop. She has not fallen to her knees or fingered a rosary, but she has an ongoing relationship with God, an attitude of prayer.

By contrast, some monks and nuns would readily—and probably humorously—admit that while they appear to be praying the Psalms, they may in fact be worrying about a dental appointment or wondering what to cook for dinner. It's usually hard to gauge an inner state by an outward appearance.

From a brief description, we may not know what's going on within the people described in the following cameos. But if they are deliberately trying to know God better, they may all represent people at prayer.

◆ the climber who reaches the peak of the 14,654-foot mountain. With legs aching, she sinks to the ground and savors a long drink of water. With full appreciation, the mountaineer looks at the surrounding peaks, frothing like waves against the sky. She smiles with wordless praise.

◆ the husband who watches beside the hospital bed of his wife. He says nothing; he holds her hand as he has for two weeks.

◆ the young woman who spends the first or last moments of the day bent over a journal. Her roommates think she's doodling; in fact, she is making sense of her life, struggling to understand the day's twists and turns, gifts and challenges.

◆ the mother who rises to nurse the baby for the third time that night. With half-opened eyes, she bumbles toward the crib, scoops up the infant, and feeds him sleepily.

◆ the student who completes a week of final exams, three term papers, a group project, and the organization of a canned-food drive. He dives into bed, but pauses for a moment before falling asleep. Words addressed to the mysterious Holy One come muffled by exhaustion: "Thanks. I got it all done."

◆ the dancer who takes a deep breath, then leaps onto the stage. As the music swells, he knows that this is the moment into which long hours of practice have poured. The dancer pirouettes and pivots with utter joy in the strength and grace of a body trained for dance.

◆ the business executive who knows that a long day looms ahead. She faces the window and lifts both hands in an eloquent gesture. "Thank you for a new day," her hands seem to say. "I am yours, O God. Help me to be kind as well as efficient."

◆ the two friends who meet over coffee to talk through a dilemma that concerns them both. They listen carefully, lean across the table toward each other, joke, respect each other's truth. They leave knowing clearly what action they must take; the caffeine was in the conversation.

◆ the protester who takes a deep breath and steps across the line at the nuclear weapons plant, thinking, "If I go to jail, I go to jail. But I can't let conscience lie down and die."

◆ the artist who launches a new project, excited about its potential while still aware that it will take many long hours to complete. Still, a tantalizing intrigue hovers over the beginning: How will this look when it's finished? What will emerge?

◆ the older sister who knows it's drudgery, but does it anyway. "Just this once, Sam," she tells her younger brother. "I'll throw your jeans in the wash with my dark load so you'll have clean

ones for the party." They grin at each other in the easy cama-
raderie of people who know they'll fail again, and once again,
they'll bail each other out.

These are fully alive human beings, perhaps not conscious of
all the implications of what they are doing, but nevertheless
deeply engaged. Some prayerful moments are as dramatic as
bounding across a stage; others as humble as laundry. The
common denominator is the spirit of the creator stirring within
the person and the human response to that voice.

These people are not praying in long, uninterrupted stretches or with precise, formal words. They might nod their heads in
agreement with Jacob's surprise: "Surely the Lord is in this
place—and I did not know it!" (Genesis 28:16). In reflection
before, after, or during the event mentioned, they might recognize God's presence and continual invitation to grow in friendship. While every action is potentially prayer, they have chosen
to consecrate theirs.

An attitude of prayer requires two parts, like two hands clap-
ping or two wings beating. Bringing God into daily life means a
constant movement back and forth between the action and the
reflection. This heightened level of consciousness characterizes
these people, and many more who are not described. Together,
they constitute a chorus of people praying even when external
appearances might not suggest it.

TOWARD A DEFINITION OF PRAYER

In a small town in the Colorado Rockies, people come to
church wearing hiking boots and cowboy shirts. They gather in

the basement to sit on folding chairs, drink coffee, and talk about prayer. As the discussion evolves, they are surprised that prayer can be so simple, so much a part of their daily routine. As people describe an ongoing conversation with God, one woman gasps, "Why, I do that all the time! How affirming to know that it's prayer!"

Jesuit priest Richard Hauser writes about his struggles to pray when he taught young students in South Dakota. Because of sheer physical exhaustion, he would sleep through the hour scheduled for morning prayer. He felt guilty about it, because daily prayer was crucial to his identity. But each night, when the dorms would quiet down, he'd go for a walk down the highway. Hauser writes, "I recall being discouraged and lonely and pouring out my heart to God. I also recall returning from these walks peaceful, feeling close to Christ and wondering how I could survive without these walks."

Then he had a startling realization: he wasn't skipping daily prayer; he was simply doing it at night. "I was walking down that highway each night to be with the Lord—not to fulfill a religious obligation. I had discovered a rhythm of being totally open to and comforted by God. I had learned to pray."[1]

Casual observers might say, "There's a guy strolling down the highway." It's highly unlikely they'd say, "That guy is praying." Yet for Hauser, an evening walk was often a more meaningful, heartfelt activity than routinely going to church and reciting rote prayers in the amnesia of early morning.

Prayer is bigger than tried-and-true formulas. It means opening ourselves to a whole splendid range of possibility. The God who created hundreds of billions of stars in our galaxy alone and an infinite number of snowflake patterns must love variety. God relishes human beings surging with life, not shadows keeling over with boredom at mind-numbing repetition. It's unlikely that God would reject a prayer because it didn't follow a particular formula.

Furthermore, God initiates the conversation. People who feel that all the burden is on their shoulders to work and succeed at prayer often feel needless anxiety and guilt. God comes to us in a myriad of ways, because God is infinitely creative about revealing God's self in ways that will best communicate with an individual. The human response is a sensitivity to God's initiative, an alertness to God's activity.

If we frame prayer as an attitude of sensitivity and openness to God, limitless possibilities are revealed: countless different styles, techniques, and rhythms are all welcome.[2]

COMPONENTS OF PRAYER

While prayer eludes strict definition, we have seen that several components are vital. Prayer is a deliberate effort to respond to God's grace in our lives and deepen our relationship. God initiates the conversation in a number of ways; we answer with alertness and sensitivity, often in a language that is wordless. Sometimes we respond to God's presence in other people, a place, or an event, knowing that God's grace is mediated by people, places, and things. The theme of prayer might be "You grace me in varied ways, my creator; I respond in my unique voice. Help me always to know you better and love you more."

The individuality of this exchange is captured in St. Thérèse of Lisieux's definition of prayer: "For me, prayer is a surge of the heart; it is a simple look turned toward heaven, it is a cry of recognition and of love."[3] Yet for seven years running, she admits elsewhere, she slept through her formal times of prayer.

Prayer is an attitude, not a formula; a journey, not a place. Jesus once asked two would-be followers, "What do you want?" In the best Hebrew tradition of answering one question with another, they replied, "Where do you live?" All seekers can be grateful that Jesus did not reply, "Fourth floor of the papal palace." Instead, he answered, "Come and see."

The staggering breadth of that invitation reminds me of my first experience of snorkeling. It was a rainy morning in the Florida Keys, the waves were roiling, and the Boy Scouts on our excursion boat had already gotten sick over the stern. When we reached the coral reef, the captain threw the ladder into the Atlantic with bravado and announced with a flourish, "Pool's open!"

Never mind that we were shivering in our wet suits or that we were clueless about our equipment. Never mind that we gauged the ten-foot waves with sheer terror. Somewhere beneath the surface, angelfish quivered through lacy violet fronds. The world under the sea awaited, abundant in beauty and hidden life. Such promise tantalizes our curiosity and calls us beyond our comfort zones.

If starting to pray is like jumping into the ocean, then jump. Come and see.

At the end of each chapter appear questions for reflection or discussion and "prayer prompts." These are intended to help the reader absorb and take ownership of the material, relate it to individual experience, perhaps discuss it with a friend or study group. They are never meant as assignments, "must do's," or mandatory work. While they may help some, they may annoy others. As with most suggestions, follow them if they help. Ignore them if they don't.

REFLECT

To the list of people "being prayer" (the climber, the husband, etc.), add your own favorite example of yourself or another person "being prayer." ◆ *Have you ever had an experience like the Colorado woman's or Father Hauser's that surprised you with some insight about the nature of your own prayer? If so, describe it.*

PRAY

Bless the beginning. If it feels natural, make some gesture such as a sign of the cross or a peaceful, enclosing circle over this book and yourself. Ask God to fill your reading and reflecting with light, challenge, and gift.

2

BETWEEN THE HYACINTH AND THE LAUNDRY PILE

Prayer as a Balancing Act

A low prayer, a high prayer, I send through space.
Arrange them Thyself, O thou King of Grace.
—THE POEM-BOOK OF THE GAEL

On a day in late February, the clutter of my room takes on symbolic resonance. At this time of year, I usually long for the beauty of flowers, so I plant hyacinth bulbs in the fall, force them, and enjoy their flowering indoors before any signs of spring surface in the outdoor garden. When one purple cone is at its peak, individual bells peel open, and the room fills with fragrance. It sings of spring, resurrection, new life. Its perfume reminds me about the importance of soul nurture. If you don't feed your soul everything you possibly can, how will you ever have any peace to give others? In similar words, Robert Wicks says, "If you don't feed your soul, you'll let your critics destroy you." The hyacinth is a feast for the senses—and the soul.

Directly opposite the flowering hyacinth is the laundry pile. Due to my recent travel, lack of time for domestic duties, and other flimsy excuses, the pile is growing high and sending forth its own unmistakable fragrance. Sweat and underwear smells blend in an aroma that the hyacinth can barely offset. It's a powerful olfactory reminder of last week's minor disasters: getting stuck in the mud, spilling coffee on a shirt, streaking the slacks with motor oil, staining the lapel with gravy.

How like human life, this little domestic contrast. In the space of three feet are symbols of the best and worst in our experience. We aspire so high; we sink so low. We are filled with great expectations and long to dance to the music of our high calling, but we fail, repeatedly and miserably, to achieve even the smallest and simplest steps. We who would be great of heart get dragged down by details; we who would soar can barely crawl; we who would sing arias can hardly croak on key. "I conceive the eagle; I give birth to the sparrow."

PRAYER POISED IN THE MIDDLE

Poised between the hyacinth and the laundry pile may be prayer. It is at once the cry of our longing to be better and the sad admission of where we really live. Prayer itself is a bold act, teetering precariously between a culture that denies its importance and a vast mystery that seems to dwarf its puny voice. Our twentieth-century, hell-bent-on-success work ethic guffaws, "What do you mean, you're wasting the first hour of the day on such a useless activity? When you could be most productive, you're sitting in silence? It's un-American!"

On the other hand, we imagine the great force that whipped the mountains into towering peaks, that filled the oceans with teeming life, that creates ongoing miracles to which we are blind. We picture a person who is the source of all compassion, whose deep peace eludes our understanding, who epitomizes all we mean by love, who gives us what we hold most precious. How could we babble an incoherent word to such a being?

Our attempt must be termed, in the phrase of African American novelist Toni Cade Bambara, an act of "sheer holy boldness." In prayer we learn both how wondrous we are and how desperately we need God. We aspire toward heaven, then watch the enthusiasm wane, the ideals dim, the human foibles slip in, the beautiful words and golden images fade. Were it not for the divine response, we might get discouraged. But what we hear in prayer from God is this: keep trying.

After prayer, we may not feel any better. We may not have rosier cheeks or a holier glow. Our unresolved problems will still loom like ugly monsters; our annoying colleague will still snort with laughter at her own limp jokes. But something inside us is different. We have a sense of being accompanied.

JESUS SHARES BOTH EXTREMES

The loudest, indeed the deafening, assurance of God's companioning comes through the incarnation of Jesus. God who took on human skin, human limitations, and human odors understands our flaws. Jesus probably created a laundry pile himself, engaged in the arduous process of getting clothes clean in the days before Maytag, and hung around with fisherfolk who were pretty whiffy in a high wind. He who loved the lilies of the field probably would have breathed a deep, appreciative lungful of hyacinth too. "Not even Solomon was arrayed like one of these," he said in admiration of field flowers. He is an authentic model for living in the spaces between—the lilies on one hand; the rancid fish on the other. His parable of the prodigal son spans two extremes—the younger son's life in the pigpen, the ecstatic moment of his father's embrace.

He doesn't qualify his invitation, "Come follow me," with an "as soon as you're perfect." Instead he lives in the thick of the messiness, not waiting till the act is cleaned up to thank God for the whole crazy, mismatched pile. He who reached out to the fringes of the human community knew sickness and stain, dirt, and the smells of humans in a warm climate before the invention of deodorant.

One of the most telling stories about Jesus comes early in his public life, and in some traditions is proclaimed on the first Sunday of Lent. After forty days of fasting in the desert, he hungers. The most natural, human condition affects him. He is not above a stomach growl. When the devil tempts him to turn stone to bread, Jesus can imagine a fragrant loaf in exquisite detail; he must long to tear into it, chewing right down the soft middle.

He resisted that seemingly innocuous temptation as he did all that followed. He refused the power and glory of the world's kingdoms, as he did the ploy to bring out God's angelic rescue squad if he threw himself from a high pinnacle. "No," he said. "No dazzling effects. No pyrotechnics. Being human is enough."

His humility speaks volumes to those of us who would have quickly grabbed any or all of those chances. (I'd be gnawing the bread; others would go for the power or prestige.) "He was so embarrassingly common and little," writes John Kavanaugh. This Jesuit commentator goes on to explain that Jesus resisted the superman techniques because they would have commandeered our loyalty. He avoided rigid control because what he wanted instead was "the free gift of a human heart."[1]

In Jesus' broad acceptance of human limits, he models prayer for us. He stands with us in the place where we say, "This is the life I have. How can I live it most fully?" We in turn don't necessarily ask how to change this life, but how to reverence it, enter it most deeply. Indeed, genuine sanctity doesn't fly off into the ether, but blesses the here and now, whatever it may be.

As Bill Huebsch explains it,

We are the ones who are spoken in prayer
and to enter into our lives
as divine in their source
and divine in their destiny

is to enter into prayer.
We are bound up with God
in such a dramatic way
that the intricacies of our lives
are filled with divine energy.
So hearing God
is hearing our lives
as they are drawn into God
in the everydayness
with which we live.[2]

To return to the original metaphor: prayer that is rooted in real life helps us keep our balance between the hyacinth and the laundry pile. Which is the high prayer and which is the low? Perhaps the sorting is best left to God.

REFLECT

Draw from your own life a metaphor that represents the two extremes of the hyacinth and the laundry pile. How do you unite the two holistically?

PRAY

I find God in the smallest detail of life, such as . . .
I find God in the lofty, significant places of life, such as . . .

3

THE INVISIBLE LINE, THE THESEUS THREAD

Prayer That Anchors

I caught [the thief] with an unseen hook
and an invisible line which is long enough to let him
wander to the ends of the world and still
to bring him back with a twitch upon the thread.

—G. K. CHESTERTON

The Father Brown mysteries were the attempt of British author G. K. Chesterton to infuse the story form with Christian beliefs and values. While the reader is absorbed in a rattling good mystery, he or she is also picking up philosophy painlessly. The stories may seem dated now, but in them Chesterton gives a helpful image for prayer: that twitch on the line by which God brings us home. On our end, we seek peace; on the other, God holds the thread.

Perhaps Chesterton's image of the invisible cord comes closest to describing that internal line connecting us with our creator, who at our conception had a dream for our lives, who knows precisely where we're going even when we're befuddled. The fact that God takes an initiative toward us may be the only logical response to the question raised by the prophet, "Who would otherwise dare to approach me? says the Lord" (Jeremiah 30:21).

To offset the risk and reduce the distance, God became one of us. Because of Christ's humanity, every human face takes on the contours of God's beloved child. The Gospels assure us, "Anyone who comes to me I will never drive away" (John 6:37). Jesus guarantees his Father, "I guarded them, and not one of them was lost" (John 17:12).

Like little kids wandering in a huge shopping center, we cling to any thread that connects us to the parent who keeps us safe. At an early age, we recognize the human person as the source of happiness, nurture, and security. As adults, we can make the same connection to God, the divine parent.

A homely analogy for this bond resonates whenever I land at an airport and try to find the shuttle bus or the ride to my destination. I used to worry that I'd never connect with the driver I was supposed to find, especially when I'd be equipped only with vague directions such as "Meet the guy wearing glasses."

Then one day, as a shuttle was ferrying me to the airport, I noticed how carefully the driver tracked arrivals and departures. The bus had three cell phones and a constant stream of communications with command post central. The driver was told exact locations, times, and names for those he should pick up. "How reassuring!" I thought. "As I search frantically, someone else, from the other end, is looking for me!"

LINES AND THREADS IN LITERATURE

In George MacDonald's fairy tale *The Princess and the Goblin,* the God-figure is a mysterious grandmother who spins a thread too fine for her granddaughter Irene to see. The little princess can feel it, however, and the slip of gossamer will protect her from the dire calamities, personified as goblins, that surround her.

When her grandmother directs Irene to follow the thread, the girl is delighted that it will lead her to the beloved figure. "Yes," cautions the grandmother. "But remember, it may seem to you a very roundabout way indeed, and you must not doubt the thread. Of one thing you may be sure, that while you hold it, I hold it too."[1]

Indeed, the thread guides Irene through perils, leads her to save another child, and returns her intact to her grandmother's beautiful arms and silver bath full of stars. What child, confronting the goblins of the playground or the dangers of the school system, wouldn't long for such a thread? What adult, dealing with more complex, sophisticated goblins, doesn't yearn for such guidance?

On difficult days, another "thread" image also reassures. At the center of the ancient Cretan labyrinth lived a monster named the Minotaur, who devoured human beings. Each year the king of Crete would send in seven Grecian women and men as tribute. None ever returned alive, until the Greek hero Theseus befriended the king's daughter. She gave him a ball of thread and told him to unravel it as he entered the maze, so that he could follow it from the center out. Theseus killed the Minotaur and escaped.

How does this story from Greek mythology relate to lives in a noisy, driven century? Many of us often feel trapped in a labyrinth we never chose, confused about where to turn next. At particularly dreadful times, we can almost hear the monster salivating.

LOST IN THE LABYRINTH

At the end of the day, with energies drained and projects still unfinished, we sometimes collapse into a sense of failure. We don't focus on all we've accomplished, but on what we haven't done. Even our best efforts weren't enough; our talents seemed wasted. In the evening exhaustion, we suspect "there's got to be more than this."

We long for an undercurrent of meaning that gives some depth to our struggles, some reason for getting out of bed the next day. Even if the boss is straight out of Dilbert, the co-workers were raised by wolves, and the family is dysfunctional, there has to be some purpose in it all. We want to live out of some spiritual center, beyond the maddening ups and downs, ins and outs that leave us restless and unfulfilled.

On a global scale, we see our personal dilemmas magnified, as if on large-screen television. Almost overnight, Margaret Thatcher's status plummets from prime minister to semi-anonymous British matron. Political fortunes can turn on a sound bite. One offhand, thoughtless comment from a sought-after speaker, and he or she is history. During the El Niño storms, million-dollar mansions along the California coast slid into the sea with little warning.

Closer to home, relationships that once seemed strong can splinter. Friends we thought we could always count on get transferred to another state. The unexpected deaths of young, vibrant people shock and depress us. Itching dissatisfaction extends even to the polo set, where designer jeans and BMWs fail to soothe heartbreak, end addictions, or restore the victims of tragedy. A roller-coaster economy creates instability in the job market; downsizing threatens even well-established corporate executives. Institutions where we once placed our trust demonstrate their unworthiness of it.

We suspect there must be more to human beings than the chorus of inner voices with their conflicting "shoulds" and "shouldn'ts," the baffling cacophony within of emotions, insights, and confusions that makes the screeching, neon-lit video arcade appear calm. There must be some guide through the days when we feel that we've just landed in a city where we don't speak the language.

In the face of our insecurities, what are our options? Cave in to the fluctuations, hoard the little we have? Or seek out something we can count on, something that endures? The first answer seems petty and greedy. To pursue the second, some people, in blatant subversion of consumerism, turn repeatedly and unabashedly to prayer. In prayer, they find a peace that doesn't depend on a good mood, an upswing in the stock market, or a sunny day. It's a freedom to move through life without all the answers, a daring act of trust, a sense of direction that can beacon through the murkiest fog, the presence of an unseen companion who gives confidence and joy.

Prayer may be the turning inward that energizes all our movement outward. One example of this shift in direction can be seen in the breathless newspaper reporting about the opening of a new shopping mall. One man eagerly waited in line for the ribbon cutting, not because he wanted to buy anything, but because he just wanted to see "what's out there." The cynics wonder if the shoppers are in desperate flight from "what's *in* there."

What *is* in there? When we hit the wall of human limitations, we look elsewhere, toward the God who at the same time is searching for us. We hunt for an invisible thread to save us.

THE SAVING THREAD

If the day is threaded with prayer, it can anchor us in a way no external stimulus can. At one time, nuns and monks punctuated the day with the Divine Office—a recitation of prayers for morning, afternoon, evening, and even the middle of the night. While that formal practice may be realistic now only in convents and monasteries, the idea is easily adaptable. For a long recitation of the Psalms, we can substitute a few lines like those below that we find particularly helpful.

Over the centuries, people have found in the Psalms a stunning variety that corresponds to all the fluctuations of human experience. Notice the gamut the psalmist runs in these brief examples. Such a range of emotions begins to describe the roller coasters we go through in an ordinary week (sometimes in an hour!). Try choosing one nugget that mirrors the mood of each day (and in turn, our relationship with God), and praying it like a mantra.

I believe even when I say, "I am completely crushed." (116:10)

What return can I make to Yahweh for all your goodness to me? (116:12)

Under God's wings you shall find refuge;
God's faithfulness is a guard and a shield. (91:4)

For you, O God, are my stronghold.
Why do you keep me so far away?
Why must I go about in mourning,
oppressed by the enemy?
Send forth your light and your truth—
they shall guide me;
let them bring me to your holy mountain,
to your dwelling place. (43:2–3)

Cannot God who made our eyes, hear?
The One who made our eyes, see? (94:6)

Too long have I lived
with people who hate peace! (120:6)

You have plunged me to the bottom of the pit,
into its very bottom.

I am crushed by your anger, drowned beneath your waves.
You have turned my friends against me
and made me a pariah to them.
I am in prison and unable to escape,
my eyes exhausted with suffering. (88:6–8)

Guard me like the pupil of your eye;
hide me in the shadow of your wings
from the onslaughts of the wicked. (17:8–9)

As for me, in my justice, I shall see your face,
and be filled, when I awake, with the sight of your glory. (17:15)

You have changed my sadness into a joyful dance;
you have taken off my clothes of mourning
and given me garments of joy. (30:11)

Maybe the cord of prayer could run through a typical day
like this:

◆ Morning: Set the alarm ten minutes early. Give God the
best time of day, before any interruptions, before anyone else
is awake.

Be filled with a thanks that can spill over into the rest of the
day. Or follow some seasonal prayer, the template of Christ's
life set over ours through the lectionary readings.

◆ Afternoon: Quit for lunch fifteen minutes early and shut the
door of the office. Pause for prayer. Or take lunch hour in a park,

alone, with a book for reflection. Or grab a sandwich, and then go for a quiet walk in which the beauty of creation can speak.

(For those who chortle at the luxury of a lunch hour, what about a pause for prayer at the stop sign, on the elevator, while waiting out the message on the voice mail, while waiting for the computer to boot up, the bus to come, or the engine to warm? No one ever said prayer had to be long to be effective!)

◆ Evening: Pause between dinner and television. Or end the day's activities ten minutes early, taking time to thank God for the day's gifts and feel the poignant absence of God in the day's down times. Remember the world's people, especially those who faced war, hunger, or oppression this day. Remember those you love, lifting them into God's care.

One of the most paralyzing things about our chaotic era is the constant threat of change. Confronting the challenge of new-ness, we may feel like stranded tourists who know neither the lingo nor the currency of the foreign land. But there again, we cling to the cord. We can move forward in trust, knowing that the past has been good . . . or if not wonderful, at least it has held traces of a loving creator's presence. After all, despite the buffets and battles, we're still alive, no? Sheer survival points to the fact that someone's rooting for us.

When we feel vulnerable and strange, we may breathe a prayer with the directness of desperation: "You made me; you got me into this; now care for me!" God's response might come in the muffled tones of a parent wakened in the middle of the night. Despite grogginess, it's a rare parent who can totally tune out the cry of a child.

Or perhaps God simply throws out the invisible cord; it's up to us, like Theseus, to pursue it—maybe blindly, maybe desperately, but knowing all the while it's the best chance we have, the only lifeline.

REFLECT

Is the metaphor of prayer as an unseen thread between God and the person who prays helpful? Why or why not? ◆ *Have you ever felt a "twitch upon the thread," or an intervention of God in your life? Describe that experience.*

PRAY

"Of one thing you may be sure, that while you hold it, I hold it too." Reflect on this guaranteed, invisible, two-way thread in terms of your relationship with God.

4

PUBLIC PRAYER

Warts and Blessings

*Now you are the body of Christ and individually
members of it.*

—1 CORINTHIANS 12:27

While much of what we've been talking about concerns prayer in private, a question may well arise about prayer in public. What about the gatherings of believers, often robust with song, that mark Sundays and feasts, funerals and weddings, births and comings-of-age?

Let's deal first with the downside, we who may incline ever so slightly toward skepticism. Let's also remember that what seems a huge hurdle to some may not even have occurred to others—and one hesitates to create mountain ranges that weren't even minor blips before. The gift of folks for whom churchgoing or public worship hasn't become a routine flattened into anesthesia is their ability to ask questions of the regulars that can help crack their Sunday stupor. Let's imagine a few of those, and possible responses.

Q & A: THE OBSTACLES

"What about hypocrisy? If I dress up in Sunday clothes and join the crowd at St. Mary Outrageous, won't I pretend to be better than I really am?"

For starters, forget the dress-up. Scratchy suits and tight shoes are relics of childhood; they may haunt the memory, but they don't linger in reality. With a few exceptions where people really *vest* for services, jeans or sweats won't cause an eyebrow to lift. In days of dwindling attendance, the attitude taken by healthy churches seems to be "What difference does it make what you wear? We're just glad you're *here*."

The hypocrisy question actually goes much deeper than dress. In the sad history of churches, people prayed so fervently while simultaneously banning people of color that it gave rise to the famous expression "The most segregated hour in the U.S. is eleven o'clock Sunday morning." In many churches today, people praise the loving creator of all, while at the same time barring women from equality.

While no defense can ever justify some church abuses, it seems safe to say that any human institution is riddled with hypocrisy. How many parents have lectured their children about good health as they smoke a cigarette and sip a martini? How many people of faith want to kick themselves routinely for an inadvertent comment that crushes another person? Human beings may aspire high, but we sometimes sink low. Why should we be any different at church?

A Trappist monk is about as regular a churchgoer as one could find, yet even Thomas Merton was revolted by a pretentious Easter service:

> The less said about the Easter morning Pontifical Mass the better. Interminable pontifical maneuverings, with the "Master of Ceremonies" calling every play, and trying to marshal the ministers into formation and keep things moving. . . . The church was stifling with solemn, feudal, and unbreathable fictions. This taste for plush, for ornamentation, for display strikes me as secular, no matter how much it is supposed to be "for the glory of God." The spring outside seemed much more sacred. . . . Sweet spring air. One could breathe. The alleluias came back by themselves.[1]

If expectations of public worship are too lofty, they will inevitably be reduced. But if we regard church as we do

Alcoholics Anonymous or Weight Watchers, our perspective becomes more realistic. People come not because they are perfect, but because they recognize their desperate need for help. In sacramental churches that center on the Eucharist, it isn't virtue that draws us there; it's hunger.

Another frequent question is, "How will I know what to do? They sit and stand on cue, but I don't have the script." So, what do you do in any new social setting? How did you figure out your first formal dance or football game? You follow the crowd, that's what you do. Surreptitiously select one confident-looking sort and mimic the actions. (Like lost drivers who inevitably ask a fellow tourist for directions, you may have glommed onto someone else who's faking. But he or she is probably shadowing someone else, and so on. See—churches are good places to get comfortable with infinity.) Many churches also provide a cheat sheet, called an order of service, or a worship aid, which prints the words of songs and prayers. Some groups have a favorite hymnal, located either at the entrance or in the pew. Pick up one with aplomb, and you look like an old hand already.

"But I feel like a spectator, not a participant!" Now you're edging closer to home. Many folks in liturgical, mainstream traditions would agree. They sit back and put the mind on cruise control while a few leaders do all the work. Can anything so passive still be prayer?

In many places, liturgy is sadly in need of reform, a fact publicized in the Catholic community by a letter of Roger Cardinal Mahony to the Archdiocese of Los Angeles. He declares the year 2000 a Year of Jubilee, a time to sort out "what of the past must be forgiven or set aside, and what of the past is worthy to be grasped and handed on, built upon, made our own and given to our children." Mahony praises the beginnings that have been made, yet acknowledges that substantial work must be done to create a "compelling and contemplative celebrating of Eucharist" every Sunday. Because people have not been well educated about the meaning of the liturgy, the distinct rites within the Mass, and the language of symbol, they have been happy with too little. They do not demand the high standards to which baptism entitles them.

If the people accomplish what Mahony proposes, and if his initiative spreads around the country, then we can look to our Sunday worship for reverence and beauty, poetry and silence, passion and festivity, flesh, blood, and spirit. It will not be dominated by the presider, but will draw forth all the cultural richness that flows from the "religious soul of a people." While liturgy should take on the "pace, sounds and shape that other cultures bring," it should at the same time be universal, spoken in the "language of Pentecost." If these high hopes are realized, people might finally stir from their stupor and "go up with joy" to God's altar.[2]

Yet having said all that, and with great expectations for liturgical reform, I realize that some folks go to church more for solace and solidarity than for stimulation. As a college professor of theology confessed, "Sometimes I go to church just hoping the hour will pass fast. Then I see the eighty-year-old mother with the retarded son, or the single parent on food stamps, and I'm grateful to them for coming week after week. I think, 'Maybe if they can hang in there, so can I!'"

She touched on what many define as the drawing card for church attendance: the community. When we see the same faithful faces week after week, we know we're not in this alone. As St. Paul puts it, "Just as the body is one and has many members, and all the members of the body, though many, are one body, so it is with Christ. . . . If one member suffers, all suffer together with it; if one member is honored, all rejoice together with it" (1 Corinthians 12:12, 26).

Over time, we learn their stories: that couple's son drowned three years ago; that woman is newly widowed; that attorney defends the indigent; that dad recently lost his job; that family helps at the homeless shelter. Many people find in their church communities a generous outreach when they need help, a place to share their joys, and a buoyancy that keeps them going when they fear that drudgery might kill their spirits. Looking around at such folk helps with the next obstacle:

"But the sermons are terrible!" While we should be cautious not to evaluate everything with North American consumer standards, this criticism is too often true. Anyone with a pulse could find more inspiration from spending a few minutes outdoors in creation than from enduring the drivel of unprepared homilists.

THE COMPENSATIONS

Yet every now and then, there's a rare exception, a talk in church that startles, surprises, confronts, redeems. It touches us where we live and echoes through the week that follows. It may persuade us to change an attitude or behavior, improve a relationship, make a decision we've been postponing. We say as we walk out, "It was worth coming just for that talk." If these bright spots happen often enough, they make all the rest endurable.

So too with the times when the liturgy is at its best and all the arts come together in praise of the creator. The right combination of music, bells, banners, dance, drama, light, poetry, fragrance, and song can move us beyond petty concerns and lift our hearts—and we find ourselves back to that classic definition of prayer, which still has a lilting appeal: "lifting the mind and heart to God."

In this realm, those of Anglo backgrounds owe a great debt to the recent effects of multiculturalism on worship that might otherwise be dry or bland. Mariachi music, African dance and preaching, Asian contemplation, Native American blessings of the four directions—all these and other influences have brought universality and vitality to a people once dubbed the "frozen chosen." The gathering of such a broadly diverse group offers hope that in Christ we who are many become one.

Sometimes a smaller group of people we know well makes the service special. We look around at old friends gathered to support a couple or welcome a new child, and in their faces we see the Christ. The warmth and spontaneity lacking in large, impersonal services sometimes spill out in small, informal services. Rigidity and confinement do not mar gatherings of like-minded people, perhaps those who have been on retreat or worked through a project together. Nothing can quite match the energy of such a gathering, which celebrates ties that have taken time to establish. We are here together because we stake our lives on the same things, seek the same face, try to measure up to the same ideals, use the same lenses for our experience. Those who stand with us reassure that we are not alone and not crazy in our pursuit of the spiritual.

Old pros at churchgoing often use time there for their own quiet meditation, prompted by what surrounds them. Writer John Shea calls it "soul wandering" when he tunes out of the action in order to absorb something he's seeing clearly. Shea describes this state: "Part of me is there, and part of me isn't. This is either a distraction [from church] or what the whole thing is about—I really don't know which."[3] Maybe those wanderings bring us closer to God than anything on the official program—and closeness to God is what worship is all about.

RELATIONSHIP OF PUBLIC AND PRIVATE PRAYER

While public prayer may seem self-conscious and pompous at times, it can in fact serve as fuel and corrective for private prayer. It energizes us to continue praying when we know that other people are doing so too, consciously trying to fashion their lives after Christ's life as we are. Our contact with motley humanity is often what we need to nudge the privatized self back to reality. A mother grumbling about a kid who can't get dressed on time eases into grateful silence when the child in the next pew throws a tantrum. The spouses irritated with each other watch quietly as a wife pushes her husband's wheelchair up the aisle. Only in church are pampered residents of the U.S., eager to get home to the TV or Jacuzzi, called to pray for the starving, warring, dying, grieving, oppressed peoples of the world.

Furthermore, if we get too squirrelly, too tangential, too self-centered in our prayer, we can count on the community to say, "That's nuts." Catholics have a name for the wonderful wisdom residing in the majority of churchgoers: they call it *sensus fidelium*, or "sense of the faithful." Pew-people may not read all the latest journals and they may not hold degrees in theology, but they know when something's cattywampus. If that something happens to be me, it's good to know they'll tell me, probably with little hedging and less politeness, that I'm akilter.

Anne Lamott speaks bluntly of the community's uncanny ability to nudge us beyond our own navels:

> *To be engrossed by something outside ourselves is a powerful antidote for the rational mind, the mind that so frequently has its head up its own ass—seeing things in such a narrow and darkly narcissistic way that it presents a colo-rectal theology, offering hope to no one.*[4]

To receive the necessary course correction, I have to be in touch with the body of faithful people, have to put in my time, if that's what it takes, in community. While church is no longer regarded as the privileged place for God—since God can be anywhere—it's still not a bad place for human expressions of grief and joy and fidelity and betrayal.

Who knows? Public prayer might inspire private prayer. It might become what it's intended to be: the impulse to go forth from church and do justice in the world. Archbishop Oscar Romero of San Salvador, murdered while he celebrated Mass, said in a 1980 homily: "This body broken and blood shed for human beings encouraged us to give our body and blood up to suffering and pain as Christ did—not for self, but to bring justice and peace to our people."[5]

Whatever else might be said about public worship, it nurtured Romero and other martyrs, Dorothy Day, and some outstanding advocates for oppressed human beings. It gave people the courage to stand for their convictions, to continue "the good fight," to do deeds that seemed impossible, and even to die for others. The church-attendance record of some of the most outstanding human beings who ever lived might cause us to think twice before we turn away.

REFLECT

What's your stance on public prayer? When does it strengthen you? When does it fail to nurture?

PRAY

I give thanks for the communities
that worship together, especially for

- ◆ *these members . . .*
- ◆ *these qualities . . .*
- ◆ *these strengths . . .*

5

THE GENUINE
THING

Prayer That Honors Reality

On the whole, I do not find Christians, outside of the
catacombs, sufficiently sensible of conditions.
Does anyone have the foggiest idea what sort of
power we so blithely invoke? Or, as I suspect, does no
one believe a word of it? The churches are
children playing on the floor with their chemistry sets,
mixing up a batch of TNT to kill a Sunday
morning. It is madness to wear ladies' straw hats to
church; we should be wearing crash helmets.

—ANNIE DILLARD

One pernicious fallacy about prayer is that it removes a person from reality. In this misperception, we pray to elude the nastiness of this world and focus on the filmy wonders of some other world. Thus, praying re-creates reality in Disney mode with religious overtones.

Some kinds of religion seem hermetically sealed, unfailingly cheery, stickily sweet, untouched by human hands. Their symbol is a perennial smiley face; the glum or grieving hesitate to introduce the shadow of sadness into their upbeat presence. Karl Rahner described their "almost naive belief in the immediacy of God and the power of the Holy Spirit."[1] Martin Marty named them the "summery" souls, who come easily into joy and dwell in "the abodes of the exuberant."[2] They exclude seekers who struggle honestly with God's absence, whose personality types are more restrained, who have what Rahner calls "a wintry sort of spirituality."[3]

The feel-good religions appeal to the human liking for black-and-white sureties, in which some people are clearly saved and others aren't. "Our camp has the right answers," these groups proclaim. "Following certain rules and regulations will lead us lockstep into a perfect heavenly mansion, thoroughly cleansed of any riffraff." They denounce the stowaways, those vulnerable and fallible human beings who somehow sneak into salvation through the cracks, by the mercy of God.

PRAYER IS NOT ESCAPISM

Those who equate holiness with scrubbed cleanliness, perky smiles, and Technicolor rainbows might be startled by the scruffiness of some saints. Many of their stories do not end happily, or in any vindication. Instead, they record failure, sorrow, mystery, frustration, aridity, disappointment. Some are known more for their quirkiness than for their clarity.

One author describes the goal of some misguided Christians:

> *They are simply on this earth to get to God in heaven after earthly life is over. Thus, their focus is otherworldly. What they do along the way is only important if it contributes to this goal; whether or not they enjoy the ride is not pertinent. The richness of the spiritual life along the way is irrelevant, merely a distraction. The purpose of life is to get there, "there" being salvation in the afterlife.* [4]

Such attitudes can be found in many denominations and at many times throughout history.

One extreme example was the cult of Heaven's Gate in Rancho Santa Fe, California, where members committed mass suicide. As Father Michael Himes, a professor at Boston College, has pointed out, their end run around being human ultimately denies what's best about being human. Their attempt to flee this sullied world is the exact antithesis of a Christianity that finds God incarnate in this time, this place, this particularity.

Luke's Gospel marks the beginning of Jesus' public life: "In the fifteenth year of Tiberius Caesar's reign, when Pontius Pilate was governor of Judaea, Herod tetrarch of Galilee . . ." (3:1). The specifics are important not because the officials were heroic figures but because Jesus was so firmly and precisely located in human history: this time, this place are holy. It's the exact opposite of "once upon a time." Salvation comes here and now, not in some far-off, ideal world or some abstract, theoretical conception.

Pieties detached from reality surface in the wild popularity of religious apparitions, whether they float over a sausage case, as Mary reportedly did in Colorado, or suggest Mother Teresa in a cinnamon roll. Although no one can comment adequately on the motivations of another human being, those who flock to such unsubstantiated visions may be missing out on a better show at home. According to Karl Rahner, God speaks a single word in prayer: the life of the one who prays.[5] If we pay attention to that voice, we begin to know how intimately, personally, and sweetly God can touch the most ordinary experience of the most routine day.

The contrast between escapist religions and the realism of Jesus may be clearer if we contrast two kinds of bread—one phony, one genuine. The difference struck me on a recent plane trip. In a rare—OK, unheard of—triumph of airline cuisine (an oxymoron), the biscotti and the coffee enhanced each other in a warm, rich blend of flavors. We of Flight 537 had lucked out at snacktime, and we knew it. As I eagerly guzzled a second cup, the man beside me requested more biscotti.

"Sorry," said the flight attendant. "Just gave the last one away. But I *could* give you a bread product." She sounded doubtful.

Instantly, I imagined it—encased in cellophane, cloyingly sweet, devoid of any nutrition—the Bread Product. It reminded me of a recent white elephant exchange, where the highlight of the party was a can labeled "Potted Meat Product." One whiff would drive anyone to vegetarianism.

Between the tawny loaf of warm whole wheat and the Bread Product stretches a chasm of difference. Only blatant deception in labeling could use the same word for the potted product as for the sizzling filet mignon (while the health-conscious now consider steak cholesterol laden, it was once—with a sprig of parsley and an aroma of charcoal—a thing of beauty).

We may be blithely unaware of how accustomed we've become to the ersatz—how many of us regularly ooh and ah over Disney's fake snow, phony mountains, and plastic palm trees? Yet few except the most spartan want to surrender our artificial lighting or our climate-controlled homes. We are so caught in the artificial that a jolt of the real takes us by surprise.

We walk in the rain, or feel a blast of fresh air across our faces, and we bolt back centuries to the way our species first lived—in touch with the seasons, their fortunes dictated by the weather, their experience of nature raw and unfiltered. While no one advocates a return to pre-penicillin days, it comes as something of a welcome shock to many folks to turn off the tube, abandon the car, or sleep beneath the stars.

If this is true in the external, physical life, how much truer it must be for the internal, spiritual life. How easily we tire of the phony masks that surround us, that we often wear ourselves. How quickly we are drawn to the authentic person, who may be slightly crazed, yet still fixes us with the direct gaze of those nothing-hidden eyes.

THE REALISM OF JESUS

Scripture holds persuasive evidence that Jesus had that rare integrity. He probably got it from his mother, who, when told she was to become the mother of God, didn't go into seclusion. Her preference seemed to be action: she made a long and grueling trip to her cousin's, which may also have conveniently and practically removed her from the clucking small-town gossip about an unmarried pregnant woman.

Jesus' story reverberates with notes of realism. In the account of his baptism, for instance, we hear the voice from heaven calling him "beloved son." The skies are torn apart, and the Spirit, like a dove, descends. After that opener, we'd expect an angel choir, a spectacular sunset, at least a harp trill. Instead we get this: "Immediately afterward the Spirit drove him out into the wilderness" (Mark 1:12). There he encounters wild beasts, loneliness, thirst, and hunger: the human condition at its most gritty.

Jesus goes on to proclaim the Sermon on the Mount, which turns human values upside down, introduces the Golden Rule and the Lord's Prayer, and offers the imagination enough fodder for a lifetime of reflection: the lilies of the field, the door on which we knock, the splinter in the eye. The narrator comments on the amazement of the people who heard this talk; we expect *Reader's Digest* to contract for reprint rights.

But what follows the lovely imagery, the clear-cut ethic, the glorious rhetoric? A whopping dose not only of reality, but of reality at its harshest: Jesus touches a leper (Matthew 8:3). He doesn't shout words of encouragement from afar; he knows how insulting a platitude would be. On the decaying, smelly flesh, his hands rest.

The same dynamic occurs after he brings a dead girl back to life (Mark 5). We'd expect some touting of the miracle, some message like "Get thee to the synagogue!" for official applause. Instead, Jesus' comment stuns in its simplicity: "Get her something to eat." He focuses on her needs, not his own. Furthermore, he's attuned to the realities of a young girl's life: she's healthy now; she has a future. So he suggests what any good Jewish mother would do instinctively: feed her.

AND HIS FOLLOWERS

In some of Jesus' followers, we see this stark realism again. To them, faith isn't a made-up world, a deluded devotion. Author and activist Dorothy Day once pleaded, "I can't bear religious romantics; I want realists." Before she fasted for peace, she visited the opera—to make sure her senses were well fed. She credits the start of the Catholic Worker movement, its service to the poor through international soup kitchens and houses of hospitality, to two words used by the co-founder, her mentor Peter Maurin. He would simply comment on what "wanted doing."

> *How I remember those two words! There's more to them . . . than any of us ever realized as we heard the expression used over and over. . . . He was telling us that we are about something larger than ourselves, that there were things that "wanted doing"—that God wanted them done. . . . But don't forget this was a leader at work; he knew in his bones how to get done what "wanted doing"!*[6]

Day's recollection of two words, weighted with meaning, contrasts with the puffery of politicians, motivational speakers, and efficiency experts, which for all its verbosity probably accomplishes less in genuine service to humanity.

In *Finally Comes the Poet*, when theologian Walter Brueggemann argues that "reduced speech leads to reduced lives," he doesn't refer to word counts.[7] He means that we who live in the flattened, deadening world of bureaucracy long for the abrasive, surprising fastball of the gospel. It breaks open a stultifying dullness and invites us to a life better than we dared to dream. If we want the sure, safe, stuffy piety, the gospel is the last place to look for it. Jesus relished stopping people dead in their tracks—as did Francis and Claire, Ignatius, Teresa of Avila, Thomas Merton, and a whole assortment of Jesus' followers. They shatter our settled realities by risking the daring reality of another order.

BECOMING PRAYERFUL REALISTS

If we take our cues from Jesus, we probably won't seek all our inspiration from a vision or surefire answers in prayer. The God Jesus revealed was a continual presence, closely involved in daily life, not a baffling deity enshrined on an unapproachable altar. With a couple of exceptions, Jesus' dialogue with God was marked not by dramatic earth tremors, but by an intense awareness, a joyful togetherness. The fact that God drew him to lonely places, often at night when most people would rather sleep, indicates that their times together held a powerful attraction. Yet their dialogue was not all sweetness and light; in a dark garden while his friends slept, Jesus prayed in agony, "Let this chalice pass."

The authenticity of these words makes them easily recognizable to the single mom on food stamps, the prisoner in jail, or the dying patient at the hospice who must look with cynicism on forms of faith that contain only cheer. To use an earlier image, they are as fake as the Bread Product compared to the stark realism of Jesus, which is as densely satisfying and as deeply nurturing as the whole wheat loaf with the crackly crust.

In a retreat house that brings buoyancy to the burnt-out, healing to the wounded, and rest to the weary, a retreatant told his director good-bye: "Well, Father, it's been great here. But now I have to get back to the real world."

To which Father replied, "That's kind of insulting, because I live here. I think maybe this is more the real world than some of the stuff we get caught up in." He must have referred to the beauty of the place, its peace, the sweep of its bedrock boulders, its simple yet moving liturgies, its quiet routines repeated daily, steadily.

He must have meant the hospitable staff, who welcome everyone as broken and expect no one to have their act together. These wise counselors are more used to the look of hunger and exhaustion in people's eyes than to the certainty of the self-appointed saviors. Maybe he alluded to the people who slide into the real thing easily, hunkering down as if for a long stay, a rightness that outlasts a few days there and carries over into all days.

A contemporary fictional character struggles with the same question of what is real. In Nicholas Evans's novel *The Horse Whisperer*, a New York editor named Annie leaves a lucrative, hectic career to find healing for her daughter and her horse in the beauty of the Rocky Mountains. There, all three are cured by a combination of "horse whisperer" Tom Booker's compassion and the peace of natural surroundings. A phone call from the East interrupts, hauling Annie back into "what she knew with dulling acknowledgement to be her real life. Though what she meant by 'real,' Annie no longer knew. Nothing, in a sense, could be more real than the life they'd found here. So what was the difference between these two lives?" She decides that one is composed of obligations; the other, of possibilities. The older one grows, the more one closes out the latter.[8]

It seems sad that Annie should discount the more "real" life with all its potential. Yet even people of deep faith can get involved in bizarre conversations about things that don't matter, in self-induced stress, in the zany fragmentation of life with kids, jobs, mortgages, co-workers, E-mail, faxes, and demands. Despite our best efforts to achieve a detached tranquility, we get caught up in stuff that may be beneath us, draining our gifts and wasting our talents. Then we find ourselves in the strange position of becoming like the pearls cast before swine.

If we find that we routinely demean ourselves, perhaps there is a place to turn. In the midst of this juggling act we call daily life, prayer can become that place where we stand face-to-face with the most important realities, quaking and trembling perhaps, but nevertheless glad to be there. Prayer can be that sacred space where the real breaks in and we know unassailably that whoever else we may be, we are God's children, loved with a fierce and reckless abandon. What movement can be easier than slipping into the presence of one who loves us?

If we spend enough time in prayer, humbly listening rather than arrogantly self-congratulating, perhaps we can learn the fidelity of Jesus. Perhaps we can grow worthy of real bread.

Daniel Berrigan stands in a long line of realistic poets when he writes:

> *Sometime in your life, hope that you might see one*
> *starved man, the look on his face when the bread*
> *finally arrives.*
> *Hope that you might have baked it or bought it or*
> *even kneaded it yourself.*

For that look on his face, for your meeting his eyes
  across a piece of bread, you might be willing to
  lose a lot, or suffer a lot, or
  die a little, even. [9]

That's the kind of bread that Jesus gave, and gives still.
Doesn't it make you want to reach for the butter and knife?

REFLECT

How do you distinguish real from unreal spirituality, the kind
that shelters us from the best parts of being human?

PRAY

Recall an experience of the "real." Savor it in your memory,
remembering its qualities so you'll recognize it the next time
such an experience comes around.

6

THE SOUL'S NATIVE LAND

The Context of Prayer

I guess he'd rather be out where the longest lines he sees
are the ones behind his skis.

—JOHN DENVER

I come from Colorado. That simple statement contains so much: the soft swish of snow beneath a turning ski, the taste of rainbow trout, the ribbon of river laid like a piece of tinsel down a valley. I moved west over a quarter century ago, in search of the beauty, the sunlight, the scope this place could give. And I've found more than I ever dreamt was there: in quiet canyons as the dawn gilds striated rock, in the fragrance of pine forests, or in the emerald color of an alpine lake. My quest has been vaguely reminiscent of *Out of Africa*, where Karen Blixen speaks of taking on the colors of the Ngong Hills—and wondering if they wear some color she has worn. I hope that people can hear in my voice the sound of waters running beneath the ice in early spring, sense the vast reaches of sky, read on my face the wonder of living in this state.

THE SOUL'S TERRAIN

But this isn't a travelogue. It simply seems that to explore prayer honestly we must look at the context from which it springs. Do people in Alabama pray differently from people in British Columbia? What about the difference between Polish and Sri Lankan pray-ers? We may never know the answer. So the question becomes, Does it matter?

For many years, I explored the theory that landscape affects literature. Could Pat Conroy have written without the shores and tides of South Carolina? Doesn't Faulkner exude the essence of the South? Would Joyce ring hollow without the pubs of Dublin? Doesn't Sandra Cisneros give unique voice to the barrio? Could Flannery O'Connor have flourished in Chicago? Didn't much of Wordsworth's inspiration come from the Lake District? Could Robert Frost be separated from New England? And in the voice of Gloria Naylor or Toni Morrison, don't we hear the sweet jazz of city streets?

Perhaps their examples suggest a close connection between the soul and its native terrain—not native as in "born there" necessarily, but native as in the place where we recognize affinity, thrive, and sink our roots. We are heirs of a Hebrew tradition that cherished home after exile in Egypt. The psalmist, for instance, cannot pray without reference to the surrounding environment: the stately cedars of Lebanon, the fire, chaff, sea, lion, wild ox, oak forest, and wilderness.

In medieval times it was said of St. Clare that when she came to San Damiano, "there she set down the anchor of her soul." Two students of Franciscan spirituality write:

> *Perhaps more so than other saints or spiritual writers the places of [Francis and Clare] seem to frame snapshots, give glimpses of the God/human, human/God intercourse.*
>
> *As one man said when overlooking Assisi, standing above it at the castle on Mount Subasio with a warm summer breeze wafting in the late evening air—and fireflies dancing on the fragrant ginestra flowers—lights from the Umbrian plain stretching gray-hued into the purple-red twilight, "Anyone could be a saint here."*
>
> *Of course, we know this statement is simplistic, but his insight is clear—there is a uniqueness to the place of Assisi and its environs.*[1]

In this century, Thomas Merton found his home in the hills around Louisville, Kentucky. He wrote:

Returning to the monastery from the hospital: cool evening, gray sky, the dark hills. Once again I get the strange sense that one has when he comes back to a place that has been chosen for him by Providence. I belong to this parcel of land with rocky rills around it, with pine trees on it. These are the woods and fields that I have worked in, and walked in, and in which I have encountered the deepest mystery of my own life. And in a sense I never chose this place for myself, it was chosen for me.[2]

It is essential to experience all the times and moods of one good place. No one will ever be able to say how essential, how truly part of a genuine life this is: but all this is lost in the abstract, formal routine of exercises under an official fluorescent light.[3]

PRAYER IN THE NATIVE LANGUAGE

North Americans, heavily influenced by Thoreau, may subconsciously seek their own Walden, their own sacred space. If a strong tie binds the soul to its locale, then prayer, the soul's language, must also be stamped with the cadence of its country. So a friend visiting from New York, delighting in the beauty of the foothills, once told me, "It must be easy to pray here. You'd just slip into it." Part of me jumped to agreement. But part of me hesitated: "Is it easier to pray here than in, say, Buffalo? If so, then God is grossly unfair."

Perhaps it's a question of letting whatever environment we're given lead us into prayer. In other words, prayer isn't some antiseptic activity that occurs in soundless, disinfected, white rooms. Prayer swells with the spices and timpani and smells and flavors and textures of creation. If it doesn't, it may seem lifeless and limp. Jesuit poet Ed Ingebretsen describes this essential sensate dimension:

Here then is prayer. In the tongues of rain.
My prayer. My blue fire.[4]

A coastal setting has shaped many of this poet's images, enters into his prayer. Rowing, swimming, tugboats, sand, waves, and piers are his language and metaphor. He tells God:

no more distant from you am I than deep
oceans are distant from the shore . . .[5]

For Ingebretsen, the compelling Christ is a fisherman courting people "as hungry and as insistent / as pelicans and gulls and terns." He speaks of his own turning to Christ:

. . . still, for need of him,
I would leave my nets to rot,
collecting salt,
along these vast and waiting shores.[6]

A COLORADO INFLUENCE

In the same way that sea salt wafts through Ingebretsen's poems and prayers, the shadow of the Rockies falls across mine. The mountains have always been a privileged place for people to seek God. When I read in the Psalms, "I lift up my eyes to the hills"; "Send forth your light and your truth—they shall guide me; let them bring me to your holy mountain, to your dwelling place"; "As the mountains are round about Jerusalem, so you are round about your people, both now and forevermore," I nod in recognition.[7]

Like most folks, we Coloradoans spend the majority of our days in cities, commuting to offices, stuck in traffic jams, shopping in malls, or driving on highways. Lest anyone think we plunk ourselves permanently on mountaintops like resident gurus, let it be known that we once lived within noxious vapors called "the brown cloud." While air quality has improved, pollutants still hang over Denver and other front-range cities; we contend with the same fumes and noise as residents of Detroit or Newark.

The difference rests on the western horizon. Even if we aren't physically in the mountains, it helps simply to know they're there. The purple, silhouetted peaks remind us that city life isn't the whole story, that driving an hour or so could bring us into another world. Somewhere in this must be an analogy to prayer: human beings aren't workhorses *all* the time, devoted to twelve hours a day of drudgery. There's more to us: a quick uplifting to the heavenly mansion or a deep descent into our inner selves transforms us into citizens of another country, ennobled and enlightened by prayer.

Perhaps people attuned to natural wonders like the sea, the prairie, or the night sky become accustomed to life on a vast scale. One look at any of these reminds us that the petty conflicts of office politics or the dreary records of banks may drag us down, but don't define us. We were made for greater things, the scope and beauty of God's creation.

PRAISING ALL CREATION

To people with such sensibilities, the torrent of water, the glow of candles, or the cascade of oil used in church settings echo the world where we are awed by waterfall, sunset, pine resin rubbed between the fingers. It's not a huge leap to a prayer that draws parallels between sunrise and the light of Christ dispelling darkness. It's easy to see how scriptural images for God can range from a boulder to an eagle, a cloud, or a vine.

Settings of natural beauty can prompt our own images for God: a sea of abundance, a field of nurture, a peak of joy, a river of compassion, a well of mercy, a sky of starry beauty. Surely it was this impulse that prompted the early explorers of this region to name the Sangre de Cristo mountains, which glowed so red at sunset that they were reminded of the Blood of Christ.

We're accustomed to surprises, here in Colorado, and I'd guess that goes for people who seek natural beauty anywhere in the world. As we hike, we know that the next turn might bring a startling vista, a new trail to explore, or a lovely lake. Those who walk the Atlantic or Pacific shores seem to look for the surprises, too: the patterns shifting light can make on water, the treasures of the tide pool, the footprints of terns on the patina of beach.

If we bring that attitude to prayer, we find surprises there as well: the sudden insight, the sense of an empty room filling with presence, a peace replacing anxiety, conviction where there was only apathy before. We come to God in trust, knowing that the origin and source of so much natural beauty and power must also hold human beings secure and continually create us. Even the destructiveness of tornado, fire, or flood brings awe: God is utterly beyond our comprehension, totally in charge of the universe as of our own small worlds.

My hikes can become a psalm of praise as I admire a lake's deep indigo tones, glistening between feathery pine boughs. The waters perfectly mirror every slim pencil stroke of aspen trunk, every hilly curve. Flowers in the riotous shadings of a Mexican market color the summer slopes. Stately purple stalks and lacy white clouds, jagged gold spikes and fuchsia nuggets create natural bouquets that the most reckless florist wouldn't risk. Whoever seeded this hillside did so with crazy abandon.

As if to accompany the stunning visual impact, the sound of cascading water is everywhere. Torrents of water pour over rock shelves, the droplets spraying a large arc and reminding us about a God of play. "God lets the breeze blow and the waters flow" (Psalm 147:18). Around quiet pools set in cool stone, little blue-and-white flowers bloom.

The classic expression of reverence for creation may be found in the book of Job. To a man agonizing over terrible losses, God speaks "from the heart of the tempest."

Where were you when I laid the earth's foundations? (38:4)

> *Who laid its cornerstone*
> *when all the stars of the morning were singing with joy*
> > *and the Sons of God in chorus were chanting praise? (38:7)*

Have you ever in your life given orders to the morning
> *or sent the dawn to its post? (38:12)*

Have you an inkling of the extent of the earth?
> *Tell me all about it if you have! (38:18)*

Have you ever visited the place where the snow is kept,
or seen where the hail is stored up? (38:22)

Has the rain a father?
Who begets the dewdrops? (38:28)

Can you fasten the harness of the Pleiades,
or untie Orion's bands?
Can you guide the morning star season by season
and show the Bear and its cubs which way to go? (38:31–32)

Who gave the wild donkey his freedom,
and untied the rope from his proud neck? (39:5)

Does the hawk take flight on your advice
when he spreads his wings to travel south?
Does the eagle soar at your command
to make her eyrie in the heights? (39:26–27)

It's heartening to hear God describing creation—no dull, academic abstractions for this creator! Apparently a conversation with God can cover mountain goats giving birth (39:1) as well as hail's barrage (38:22) and lightning's forks (38:24).

To this brilliant display of embarrassing questions, Job responds with the humility of one who has seen God in the lightning and thunder. We of the twentieth century are sometimes tempted to the arrogant assumption that our scientific knowledge and advanced technology can control everything. We might do well to learn Job's words to God:

I know that you are all-powerful:
*   what you conceive, you can perform.*
I am the [one] who obscured your designs
*   with my empty-headed words.*
I have been holding forth on matters I cannot understand,
*   on marvels beyond me and my knowledge. . . .*
I knew you then only by hearsay;
*   but now, having seen you with my own eyes,*
I retract all I have said,
*   and in dust and ashes I repent. (42:1–6)*

This awareness of our own limitations is reinforced by a mountain landscape. We spend a lot of time hiking uphill and have aching calf muscles to prove it. Beyond the physical effect must also be a psychological one: we know that life is a journey. *Process*—not *arriving*—is the crucial thing. While we may scale one peak, there are always more mountains to climb. Life doesn't have to be perfect to be holy; our high country offers a constant invitation to keep climbing.

Human beings are always fascinated by threshold points: where sea meets land, earth meets heaven, or human meets divine. Mountains wash against the sky, and jagged peaks poke holes in soft scarves of clouds. Whenever we're tempted to make our problems, our obsessions, or our homes the center of the world, we need only lift our eyes to the horizon. Smelling the snow melting in warm sun, marveling at the vast sweep of unfolding terrain, we remember the phrase that anchors our yearning: "Christ, the desire of the everlasting hills."

REFLECT

Where do you live? How do you think the place you live affects your prayer?

PRAY

Using my surroundings as a starting point, I pray . . .

7

THE TROUBLE WITH PRAYER

And Some Solutions

*Dear God, I think about you sometimes even when
I'm not praying.*

—ELLIOT

Prayer is full of pitfalls, but Elliot, a child on the Internet, has neatly avoided one: self-consciousness. Sometimes we see prayer as nervously racking up good-kid points, pasting gold stars in some cosmic grade book. The smug look of relief that occasionally crosses the faces of people leaving church almost shouts, "Whew—that's done. Now—on with the day!" To them the demarcation is clear: at the doorsill of church, prayer ends. "Real" life begins. Prayer is a chore and an obligation, endured because it's vaguely beneficial for moral fiber, like a dental cleaning or a tax form. Put in the time; get a pat on the back, this thinking runs.

Logic must question this regimented approach. If prayer is regulated and enforced, can it still be spontaneous communication between lovers? If it's an exercise in self-congratulation, is it authentic? Can a neatly compartmentalized slice of life that meets a requirement be genuine? If prayer is confined to church on Sunday, how can it affect the rest of the week: the lawn mowing, errand running, sandwich eating, work doing that constitute most of our days?

The inveterate pray-er and immensely practical St. Teresa of Avila adds a further complication. She believes that the only real prayer leads to action intended to honor God. She is scathing in her criticism of pseudo-prayer: "a handful of consolations that do nothing but console ourselves."[1] In her metaphor, prayer is like the water a gardener pours on flowers. The flowers are the virtues; the purpose of prayer is nurturing them.

In addition, she points out that those who suffer pray by offering their pain to God. Although Teresa predated inclusive language, she knew the genuine from the phony. Often the person who suffers "is praying more truly than one who goes away by himself and meditates his head off, and, if he has squeezed out a few tears, thinks that is prayer."[2]

Even more difficulties arise if we think of prayer as asking favors. Does God randomly dole out blessings to some and withhold them from others? Would we want to have much to do with a God capricious enough to be manipulated by pleas, so that one child in a hospital bed recovers and one in an adjoining bed dies? Would we want to pray if we equated prayer with a bribe that outdoes the Mafia's machinations?

The troubles with prayer are multiple, then. Prayer resists being turned off and on like a tape player. It cannot be regimented or legislated. It cannot be the self-absorbed, false effort Teresa describes as eking out a few tears and impressing skeptics. Nor can it be a desperate human effort to placate or motivate an angry, distant deity.

SOME SOLUTIONS

Many people who have thought long and hard about prayer (and prayed a lot) don't seem paralyzed by these difficulties. Indeed, they suggest solutions to all the problems mentioned. For them, prayer seems unselfconscious, a matter of sinking into God, becoming at one with God. Poet Jessica Powers describes this "disappearing act" into God: "I walked out of myself and into the woods of God's mercy and there I abide."

People who repeatedly try to be at one with God, to discover again and again their union with their maker, find that no matter what happens, they can go through it with grace. Their prayer seems to be a constant immersion, a burning awareness that what's human is holy and that what seems insignificant is bathed in divinity. Their prayer is a deliberate movement to the quiet pool of the inner self where I meet the God who is lover-creator-friend. The French phrase *je me souviens* means "I remember," but more literally, "I return to myself," and in so doing, to the source of my life. Such prayer can be all-pervasive, a persistent habit of finding God's presence everywhere.

Can we really pray everywhere? Even in the emergency room? the retirement center? the jail? the bar? the traffic jam?

That legitimate question deserves a clear answer. Many theologians would say that God continues to create everything, and divine energy pulses through all creation. If God abandoned something, it would no longer exist. Hence God is in everything, no matter how odd the setting seems. The examples that follow are deliberately drawn from difficult places: not quiet chapels, but a prison, nursing homes, a concentration camp.

PRAYER IN TOUGH SPOTS

Take a worst-case scenario: the corridor leading to the death chamber. In the film *Dead Man Walking*, based on Sister Helen Prejean's actual experiences, she transforms that gray tunnel into a place of inspiration and encouragement. She reads to the condemned killer a passage from Isaiah:

When you pass through the waters, I will be with you;
and through the rivers, they shall not overwhelm you;
when you walk through fire you shall not be burned;
and the flame shall not consume you. (43:2)

Shackled and fearful, the condemned man nevertheless stumbles toward the electric chair in a frame of mind that has mysteriously been lifted into God. There must be some connection between the prayer and his asking forgiveness in the last few minutes of his life.

Another difficult spot is the nursing home. Some people dread the odors, the slumped figures in wheelchairs, the hulls of human beings from whom life is draining away. Yet the attitude of these people can transform the place into a scene of great joy. Pat Livingston tells of visiting an elderly nun who welcomes her visit as proof of a gracious God, even more meaningful because all they'd had for dessert that day was green Jell-O. "Ah," she sighs. "To have you visit on such a day! La délicatesse du Bon Dieu."

Kathleen Norris tells a similar story in her book *The Cloister Walk*. She was nervous about visiting an elderly priest who had fallen down and hurt himself badly. She worried about disturbing a man who might be sleeping or in pain, but admits her surprise: "Nothing could have prepared me for what happened." When a nurse announced a visitor, Norris heard the monk's weak voice, "Ah . . . it's a sweet life." His face was "hideously bruised," but "he radiated the love of Christ" and gave the author "words I didn't even know I needed—'It's a sweet life.'" Norris concludes, "When we're at a low ebb, sometimes just to see the goodness radiating from another can be all we need in order to rediscover it in ourselves."[3]

Etty Hillesum, a courageous prisoner in a Nazi concentration camp, vividly described "the web of sorrow" surrounding her. "Could one ever hope to convey to the outside world what has happened here today?" she once asked a companion.[4] If anyone could, it was Etty. In "Letters from Westerbork" she translates the numbing figure of six million Jews into individuals who awaken our compassion: the "court jester who looks like death warmed up," an old man reciting the Shema as he dies, a little girl whose "face has disappeared, she is all eyes," the "blank and brutal despair" of the young mothers, or the "tiny piercing screams of the babies, dragged from their cots in the middle of the night."[5]

Yet if we look at the whole story (recorded in her diary), we see emerging in Etty's prayer life before her imprisonment the threads that would carry her through its horrors. Clear-sightedly, she names the evil of the death camp: "So that's what hell is like."[6] In the ancient tradition of Jewish people who had no qualms about shaking their fists at God, she asks, "'God Almighty, what are you doing to us?' The words just escape me."[7]

The habit of prayer had prepared Etty for the worst. Before her incarceration, she anticipated with deadly seriousness the ugliness that lay ahead. Yet she transformed her crushing anxiety: "Once you have begun to walk with God, you need only keep on walking . . . and all of life becomes one long stroll— such a marvelous feeling."[8]

This conviction of God's companionship sustained her throughout the ordeal. Confined behind barbed wire, sleeping on the bare board of the third bunk, shocked by brutality, undernourished and exhausted, she nonetheless writes, "Against every new outrage and every fresh horror we shall put up one more piece of love and goodness, drawing strength from within ourselves."[9] Looking back over her life, close to her death at age twenty-nine, she sees it unfolding in terms of prayer: "What a strange story it really is, my story: the girl who could not kneel.

Or its variation: the girl who learned to pray. That is my most intimate gesture, more intimate even than being with a man."[10]

OUR OWN PRACTICE OF PRAYER

These examples of people who brought God's presence into the worst settings may seem unusual. But if we anticipate the inevitability of finding ourselves in painful circumstances someday, wouldn't we want to be just as graced and gracious? Will we ever pray *there* unless we first pray *here*, in the ordinary settings of office or home?

For example, let's say that morning prayer focuses on the line "The earth is full of the mercy of God." We might dismiss that Psalm verse as an empty piety if we don't test it against our experience. So as the day evolves, we look for evidences of that mercy. The instances may seem minor: someone else cancels an appointment, so we can get a haircut. The new tennis racket we've been pining for goes on sale. The job we've procrastinated about starting gets canceled. The three drops of gas left in the tank get us to the station. Someone who really shouldn't have forgiven us does. Events conspire so that two friends who haven't seen each other in a long time can meet for dinner. A delay in leaving the office means catching an important phone call.

It's all a dance of tiny steps, but they add up to a whole pattern of beautiful movement. Or to use another metaphor, each instance may seem like a minuscule drop, but taken together, they become a tidal wave of mercy, bathing and blessing us. Awareness seems crucial; it is mentioned so often by spiritual writers that it becomes a refrain. Are we alert to the mercies that fill our days? We may not recognize them as they come suddenly, hidden or camouflaged, but in retrospect they become clear. Confronting massive evidence, we think often and gratefully of God, the great instigator.

Maybe Elliot's onto something. The temptation to self-congratulation or groveling never clouds the waters when we simply think about God. That activity isn't in the running for awards or points or prizes. Those who think about God don't have another agenda; they move in a still center of awareness, graced by presence. Maybe learning to pray is simply part of a larger learning to be.

REFLECT

The thing that troubles me most about prayer is . . . ◆
One time when I was able to pray during distress was . . .

PRAY

*Good and gracious God, when I simply think about you, this
is what comes. . . .*

8

PRAYER AND TEMPERAMENT

Adapting Prayer Styles to

Personality Types

For as in one body we have many members, and not
all the members have the same function, so we, who
are many, are one body in Christ, and individually
we are members one of another. We have gifts that
differ according to the grace given to us.

—ROMANS 12:4–6

Sarah and Meg are close friends, but their friendship is one of the few things they have in common. Temperamentally, they couldn't be more different. Sarah ponders decisions for a long time; Meg makes them quickly, impulsively. Sarah draws energy from time alone; Meg thrives on large, noisy crowds. When they go to the beach together, Sarah goes for a solitary walk along the coast; Meg spends time in the shops and cafés along the boardwalk, people watching. Sarah's idea of a fine evening is a good novel, an intense conversation with one friend, or a new video. Meg is on the phone as soon as she gets home from work, lining up an evening of dancing or partying with friends.

By now, most people are somewhat familiar with the basic characteristics that distinguish the introvert (Sarah) from the extravert (Meg). In offices and classrooms around the country, people familiar with the Myers-Briggs Type Indicator (MBTI) and the Enneagram come to a better understanding of their colleagues, classmates, and students. These tools identify patterns of action and temperament that help account for the differences in people. They help us understand ourselves and others better.[1]

THE MYERS-BRIGGS TYPE INDICATOR

The MBTI provides a "shorthand" to identify different personality types:

An extravert (E) is a person who turns to other people as a source of energy. The introvert (I) recovers in solitude the energy that other people drain. The distinction describes *preference*: of course extraverts like to be alone, and at times introverts enjoy company. But for the most part, the former chooses breadth, the latter depth; the former external events, the latter internal movements; the former interaction, the latter concentration. In this country, extraverts make up about 75 percent of the population, introverts about 25 percent.

A sensate preference (S) means that a person wants facts, practical experience, sensible, actual happenings. The "sensible" person (75 percent of the population) notices details and values the wisdom of the past. An intuitive person (N) finds appeal in innovation, metaphor, dreams, and imagery. He or she acts on intuitions and is intrigued by the possibility of the future. Intuitives comprise about 25 percent of the population.

People who are more comfortable making choices on a personal, relational, values-driven basis are called the feeling types (F). This is the only category that seems to be influenced by gender; six out of ten women report this preference. More men than women (six out of ten) report the thinking preference (T); that is, they make decisions based on objective, logical principles.

People who like to keep things open and fluid are the perceiving types (P). They like to gather lots of information before making decisions and regard deadlines as "more a signal to start than to complete a project." The judging types (J) like closure and push toward decisions; they take deadlines seriously.

Once people have established their preferences in each of these four areas, they then run the string of initials together; so someone might refer to herself as an "ENFP" or an "ISTJ." This brief overview cannot consider the subtleties of the different personality types, but often people will recognize themselves immediately when they read descriptions of their own types. Suddenly they understand that they are not alone, that they are not strange. They are simply different, and the tool helps them appreciate the wide variety in human beings.

So how does all this knowledge influence prayer? Doesn't it make sense that Sarah and Meg, who approach almost everything differently, would bring their unique personality types to prayer?

ONE SIZE DOES NOT FIT ALL

In prayer as in everything else, one size doesn't fit all. Sarah, for instance, tells the story of attending a Taizé prayer service with a friend. Sarah had resisted the idea for months, although she was curious about the repeated chanting and the wide influence of the ecumenical monastery in Europe. So she finally caved in to pressure from her friend, who pleaded, "Please come! You'll love it! You'll feel so peaceful afterward!"

But Sarah felt uncomfortable. The presence of many other people distracted her from praying; she longed to be at home alone in her familiar "prayer chair," with the fountain and flowers she had carefully arranged nearby. She found the chanting of repeated words monotonous; the "mantras" that had brought her friend peace brought her only boredom. While Sarah thanked her friend pleasantly for the experience, she vowed never to repeat it.

A similar situation occurred when Hannah persuaded her husband to join her for centering prayer. Matt was startled to discover that he was expected to sit in silence for an hour—and pay a donation to do so! While it may have worked for his wife, it definitely wasn't his style of prayer. Matt wanted direction, someone to take him through a process, some prayer or song voiced in common.

People who once learned a uniform style of prayer may be surprised to discover not only a smorgasbord of prayer types, but also their intimate connections to individual temperament. This discovery can be freeing; it opens avenues to holiness that are unique to each of us and destroys stereotypes of what constitutes prayer. No more apologies because the latest prayer fad doesn't work; no more misperceptions that the only way I can be holy is to be like Sister X or Reverend Y.

One caveat, though: in order for this knowledge to be as freeing as it should be, we must be wary of enshrining it. Once people have identified their personality types, the categories can become too narrow. We can settle into the cage defined by the Myers-Briggs or Enneagram and forget that most adults are flexible. Through the socialization process we've learned to adapt. A high extravert like Meg has learned to value silent retreats; a dyed-in-the-wool introvert like Sarah has been drawn out of self by family, job, or friends.

PRAYER TYPES

Experts have defined four major prayer types to which most of us are attracted. It's somewhat unnerving that the four types have been named for men. The exclusively masculine names make it harder for women to relate, so to balance the scales a bit, all four of the following prototypes are female.

Thomistic/NT: Ina

After a long, successful career as a professor of philosophy, Ina was recently promoted to the presidency of the college. An excellent administrator, she manages time efficiently, and often controls more details of *their* lives than her friends would like!

To ensure the smooth running of the school, Ina fired several people who had become "deadwood." While Ina did not relish the task, she knew it was necessary to maintain high standards. Despite a packed schedule, she still teaches an honors seminar for philosophy majors, because her students are a link to the future and ask questions that keep her on her toes.

Intellectuals, high achievers, and leaders constitute a group that gathers information intuitively and makes decisions based on logical analysis. They are gifted with "a concern for justice, an understanding of theology, a passion for truth."[2] They hold in contempt stupidity, carelessness, and mistakes. Their patron saints are Teresa of Avila and Thomas Aquinas, both known for brilliant, carefully reasoned books, *The Interior Castle* and the *Summa Theologica*. A charter member of the "Thomistic" group, Ina's favorite form of prayer is "lectio divina." She likes its orderly progression of four steps: reading a Scripture passage, meditating to discover God's message within it, praying over it, and contemplating. From the insights gained during her meditation, the next step is practical implementation in life. To stretch her habitual style, she sometimes takes an afternoon off, drives to a nearby lake, and "smells the roses" like a regular Franciscan.

Augustinian/NF: Erica

Erica is so intuitive she can tell what's bothering her friends and family and often predict what they'll say before they say it. While her husband goes through a long, linear process of reasoning, Erica can arrive at the same insight almost instantaneously. In school, teachers were puzzled why she could never demonstrate her line of thinking. Erica was equally puzzled why they went through so much trouble to reach the point she could attain almost effortlessly; their long proofs and processes bored her. She turned instead to her personal relationships; in friendship she found strength and gave graciously of herself.

Erica likes to journal and finds this record a help in her spiritual life. She relates to the advice once given to poet Anne Sexton: "God is in your typewriter." She is intent on finding meaning in her life and deepening her relationship with God. Whenever Erica hears about a soul thirsting for God, she nods in agreement. Because she is so intuitive, she understands the language of symbol and has a strong sense of mystery and holiness. To stretch her prayer style, she sometimes prays spontaneously, and she is learning to live with her own imperfections.

Franciscan/SP: Dotty

Dotty volunteers at a soup kitchen, and her garage is the depot for clothing, books, and toys she collects for migrant children. Like Dorothy Day, who founded the Catholic Worker movement and devoted herself to the needs of the poor, Dotty finds her prayer in service. She likes action; she excels at hands-on activity, crisis intervention, organization, and negotiation.

Researchers identify Dotty's prayer style as Franciscan. They name Mother Teresa of Calcutta and Father Damien of Molokai as saints who have followed the path of "faith in action."[3] Dotty is attuned to her inner spirit and wants to follow it freely. A tightly structured approach or a boring routine drives her crazy. She finds God's beauty in creation; St. Francis's Canticle of the Sun is a perfect expression of this style. Centered in the present, her prayer makes ample use of all five senses. Because her work is truly her prayer, she may need and set aside less time formally defined as prayer than Erica does. But her sister gave her a journal for Christmas; every now and then, Dotty expands her style by writing in it.

Ignatian/SJ: Carla

When a retreat leader introduces a meditation, asks participants to close their eyes, and invites them to enter a Scripture reading imaginatively, Carla is right at home. Her spirit responds; she quickly visualizes herself walking the dusty roads of Judea, smells the aromas of the Jerusalem marketplace, or tastes the salt spray as her fishing boat plies the Sea of Galilee. Her identification with the characters in Gospel stories enables her to understand how they related to Jesus. Quickly she can empathize with the widow of Luke 7:11 or the father of the boy possessed, Luke 9:37–43. By creating these imaginative relationships, she comes closer to Christ.

Carla values order, practicality, and service. Like St. Elizabeth Ann Seton, she is a teacher, loyal to her school and her tradition. She likes to pray as the ancient Hebrews did, by placing herself in a historical event such as their liberation from Egypt, reliving and participating in it in her imagination. When Carla goes on retreat, she follows some form of the Spiritual Exercises, enjoying its rather tight structure (which would make Dotty crazy). A good friend who understands Carla's dedication to schedules sometimes encourages her to do something unplanned and open-ended, which helps her laugh at her usual lack of spontaneity.

While the preceding sketches are brief enough to be manageable, they are also short enough to be shallow. Those who are interested in personality type as it affects their prayer life will surely want to read more; those who are just beginning this study will want to take the Myers-Briggs instrument and/or determine where they stand on the Enneagram. An abundance of resources is available on both, but one of the few books that addresses the connection with prayer is *Prayer and Temperament* by Chester Michael and Marie Norrisey, from which much of this material is drawn.[4]

REFLECT

With which personality type and prayer style do you identify most strongly? Are there others to which you can also relate? ◆ *Do you find the connections between prayer and temperament freeing or restricting? Why?*

PRAY

If you identify with the Thomistic style, reflect on a virtue such as kindness. Think of times you have been kind, or failed to be kind. What changes do you need to make to be more kind? What kindness could you do today? Conclude with a prayer to the saints who were known for this virtue, asking for their help. ◆ *If you identify with the Augustinian style, read John 17 slowly and reflectively. Insert your name when possible, and imagine Jesus praying this prayer for you.* ◆ *If you identify with the Franciscan style, meditate on a waterfall, a starry sky, a flower, a forest, a sunset, or some other wonder of nature. Create your own canticle of* praise, similar to St. Francis's. ◆ If you identify with the Ignatian style, imagine yourself in the parable of the good Samaritan (Luke 10:25–37) or prodigal son (Luke 15:11–32), taking the roles of different characters in each story. ◆ A word of caution: many people identify with more than one type. That's fine—we human beings are infinitely complex and shouldn't rule out any helpful possibility.

9

ORDINARY TIME

Praying the Texts

of Our Lives

. . . enchanted by the patterns in the haphazard . . .

—EAVAN BOLAND

Mention regular prayer to some folks, and get the polite, quizzical look. Many people regard one who prays as pleasantly eccentric, probably given to out-of-body experiences or levitation. In a world such as ours, given to pleasure and fed by hype, the person who turns to regular prayer must be an escapist, scanning the skies or floating on clouds. Some people assume that the place of prayer is an antechamber to La-La Land.

THE STUFF OF OUR DAYS

Instead, what leads to prayer is in fact the stuff of our days— the regular diet, not the occasional cake. Those who pray are also those who take this world quite seriously. They see beyond its pleasures to its less-than-rosy pits. They deal not only with the beautiful, the bright, and the healthy, but also with the physically diseased, the criminal, the mentally unsound. One suspects that it's the power of prayer that keeps them returning to the jails, hospitals, counseling offices, and hospices without the burnout that afflicts many in the caring professions.

The risk for those who pray, and those who wish we prayed more, is that we may rely on external sources such as books, authority figures, or worship services as the only ways to begin prayer. We may overlook what is close at hand, particularly tailored by God to fit our particular size and shape. If we believe that prayer is a dressy event, for which we vest in alb or prayer shawl, then the clothes we wear daily may seem too shabby or casual, too ill-fitting or uncomfortable for prayer. But if we believe that every experience comes from God's hand, then each one can become material for meditation.

Joan Chittister, an authority on Benedictine spirituality, says:

If I really believe God is present in my life, here and now, then I have no choice but to deal with that. Life, in fact, will not be resolved for me until I do. No manner of other agendas will ever completely smother the insistence of the God agenda. No amount of noise will ever successfully drown out the need to discover what is most important among all the important things of life. No degree of success will ever feel like success until I am succeeding at the center point of life. [1]

To put that in more direct terms: If I am here, in this particular sequence, with these particular people, in this particular place, why? Or, to address the question to God: You've got me where you want me. Now what do you want me to learn? Becoming my best self may not mean an efficient, businesslike process of dictating goals and ticking off achievements. It may mean paying attention to what God is doing in my life, heeding the stirrings and changes and gifts and voices and challenges and interruptions of each day, because (we presume) God knows what God is doing.

FOR EXAMPLE, A MOVIE

Let's take a simple example: we see a movie. Of all the vast selection of movies, we choose this one at this time. (That may be more complicated than it sounds, given friends' lack of agreement on which one to see, scheduling conflicts, reviews, prices, sold-out signs, etc. So a combination of factors brings us to this movie at this time.)

Let's make a further presumption: it's a good movie. (Because if it's horrendously stupid, this discussion grinds to a quick halt. Not that God can't be found in bad movies too, but let's make this easier on ourselves.) Anyway, it's such a good movie that it resonates into the week that follows. We find ourselves remembering classic lines, thinking about provocative characters, wondering about the ending. We appreciate one character's commitment to her art, another's dedication to his son, another's sense of humor. If the villains are well drawn, we catch a glimpse of their humanity and realize that few people are pure evil straight through.

Perhaps it's a leap, but we look on these characters, as we do characters in fiction, with some of the empathy the actor or author must have had. We start looking at the odd lot of people who surround us, wonder what in their past brought them to this point and made them so irritable or so gentle. This may be the longest leap of all, but we're talking about grace here: in some degree that is impossible to measure, this movie helps us share in the compassion of Christ, in God's tender involvement with the creatures God created.

"All that from a movie?" some might scoff. Ah, remember the source. Surely it was God who brought us to that movie in the first place, given all the variables, all the countless other possibilities. And who says God can't work through Hollywood? Perhaps we learned something from that movie that we couldn't learn as effectively anywhere else.

Such an approach (to a movie as to any life experience) presupposes a thoughtful stance: we don't just gobble it down as we do the popcorn and forget it an hour later. We try to mine our experience as Mary did, she who "treasured all these things and pondered them in her heart" (Luke 2:19).

PAUSE TO REFLECT

Often, events come too fast and furious for thoughtful reflection. So we pause later in the day to ask, What did that phone call from a friend do for me? What was that argument really about? We might thank God for the energy that came from coffee or lunch, the merciful cooling in a heat wave, diversion of a storm, or waiving of a deadline. Nor do we neglect the negatives. Questions such as Why do I feel so bitter or depressed? What is drawing me away from God? are as important as asking, What brought me closer to God today?

Theory without examples can become lifeless or airy, so let's look at a few days in one person's life. They are atypical because they occur during a weekend, but a more leisurely time lends itself better to reflection. They are also limited by the lifestyle of the author, a middle-class mom who lives with school-age children near the Rocky Mountains. Without further apologies, let's plunge into the weekend.

WEEKEND SCENARIO

The family has prepared and saved for a ski trip so long that nasty weather can't change the plans. So they ski all day in driving snow, which is not as bad as it may sound. The temperature is fairly warm; their clothing is protective. From the silence of the blizzard comes a deep peace. Voices are hushed; crowds decrease; fresh powder muffles noise. As the mom makes easy turns into silken banks, she feels a happiness that cannot be explained in words. It is gift of a generous God, sent freely as snow.

The next day is brilliantly sunny, and Mom delivers kids to the slopes with a sigh of relief. Then she races back to pack up the suitcases and food boxes that clutter the hotel room.

Finally, she collapses in a chair by the swimming pool. Sinking into reflection, she ponders the odd combination of circumstances that have brought her to this moment. She asks herself, Why did I ski yesterday and not today, which in many ways would have been better?

She answers: Because I would have missed that quiet world shrouded in snow, that turning deeper and deeper into mystery which became an image for the bottomless compassion of Christ. Because I might have missed the scope of the divine architecture that hurtles blizzards across vast reaches and softens granite with satin. Why do I sit now in sunlight, while wind tousles the pines and white peaks scrape the sky beyond the windows?

Perhaps some learnings do not bear the awkward encumbrance of words. Maybe God works like an architect who lays a foundation that emerges only later, in some heightened empathy for one who needs it badly, or some tranquility in the midst of chaos. I do not know now how these experiences will unfold in time. But the next rung up from not knowing is faith. In a process of conversion that is never complete, I learn to let God be God. Funny how we question that—as if it weren't enough.

MONDAY ROUTINE

The next day in the city should mean back to work, a brisk resumption of Monday routine. But one child is sick, probably from too much skiing in bad weather. She coughs and runs a fever high enough to keep her home from school. A few phone calls to the office rearrange the day. Relishing an extra holiday, Mom crawls back into bed with a Joan Chittister book, hoping to read about Benedictine humility.

She gets no further than "There are . . . other ways and other answers and other plans than mine that obviously bear recognition if I am to grow beyond myself and come to appreciate the beauty in others."[2] The rest of the day seems designed to teach her the wisdom of that sentence. A phlegmy call for help ends the reading and starts the real learning.

For a sick child needs attention: lozenges and orange juice and back rubs and stories and clean pajamas and lots of wasted time. She will not be deflected with half-attentions. She could be St. Benedict's best teacher's aide. This will not be the day Mom reads the book, writes the article, unpacks the suitcases, or cleans the house. The alternate agenda begins with snuggling in to read *Winnie the Pooh* together. A bear of little brain may miss the jokes and nuances, but he is a fine guru for humility. He may eat the honey meant for Eeyore's birthday present, but he recoups by salvaging the jar and making it the gift.

More important than Piglet or Roo is the soothing voice that wraps the child in security and settles her for a nap. As any parent would attest, no academic degree, no achievement in the world equates to a temperature drop on the fever thermometer or the healing sound of relaxed breathing. That fading fever and ensuing pause must be God-given: Mom gets a chance to catch up on work, make a few phone calls, answer some E-mail, and reconnect to the human race.

But there's little time for thanks as other children arrive home from school famished and the evening falls into the usual cooking, dinner, homework, and laundry routines. An ordinary day? Yes and no—reflection reveals glimmers of gold thread in the fabric.

WHERE'S GOD?

Where was God in the day? Surely God was present not only in the few minutes officially marked "prayer." The spiritual reading was quickly interrupted, but God is not constrained by human notions of prayer. The chapter on humility continued as Mom discovered her limitations, her simple but soaring achievements, her gratitude to the divine healer.

The challenge now is not so much to dwell on one person's experience as to plumb what is uniquely personal. Because those experiences vary widely, a few general questions may start the process. Reflecting on these may help us see what stories God is writing in the texts of our lives.

◆ Where are the seeds of the sacred sown in an ordinary day?

◆ Where does God make surprising breakthroughs, in disasters reversed or extraordinary kindnesses?

◆ Where does grace splash the surface of routine?

◆ How do the negatives challenge us to grow, or push us to a wall where we see how much we need God?

◆ How is the seemingly haphazard in fact sublimely patterned?

REFLECT

Reading the text of your life, where do you find God?

PRAY

Today I met God in . . .

10

FLUENT IN MANY TONGUES

The Languages of Prayer

Since when are words the only acceptable

form of prayer?

—Dorothy Day

Oh, dear. Must the words of prayer be fussy, formal, full of *thees* and *thous?* For God to hear, do we need to speak like courtly Renaissance bards or Victorian poets? Need we invoke the Deity as would the pope or the archbishop of Canterbury in brocaded regalia, backed by the lace-clad choir? To all of the above, a resounding Nope.

While it's easy to say what the language of prayer is not, it's harder to define what it is, because that varies widely from person to person. What follows, then, is not necessarily the Be-All and End-All Definitive Guide. Your own particular favorite may not even be mentioned. All the more reason to pursue it, develop it, savor it. While some qualities of prayer language are universal, others are distinctly personal.

SOMETIMES THE LANGUAGE OF PRAYER IS FORMULAIC

For many people, prayers memorized in childhood are helpful: the Lord's Prayer, the Hail Mary or Memorare, the rosary, a whole range of devotions. For those whose childhoods didn't include such lessons, or those who've forgotten, prayer books are easily obtainable in bookstores or libraries. More recent collections such as Desmond Tutu's *An African Prayer Book* present a multicultural approach to prayer; Ed Hayes's prayers in *Prayers for a Domestic Church* and *Prayers for a Planetary Pilgrim* range from the domestic sphere to the planetary scope; Miriam Therese Winter's prayers in *Woman Word, Woman Song* are tailored especially for women; and Joyce Rupp, in *May I Have This Dance?* and many other books, sets her prayers to music and creates simple chants.

Obtaining the words is easy; the tough part is taking ownership of them. People can usually do it in a crisis: when the plane
starts going down, passengers mumble "Angel of God, my
guardian dear," grace before meals, an act of contrition, a creed—
anything they can remember on the spot. Before patients go into
surgery or while relatives wait outside intensive care, they comb
books or memories for appropriate words to pray.

During these states of siege, it's often helpful to have a stock
of memorized phrases that have helped before and can be
counted on to help again. When emotions are drained, the situation is tense, or the body is exhausted, it's tough to be original
and creative, so we turn to what's close at hand. For centuries,
people repeated the rosary because they found it soothing or
calming. When we are too sick, too old, or too tired to conduct
research on new prayer forms, the tried-and-true standbys
come to our assist. Then we may be grateful for the Psalm we
memorized, the words that spring easily to mind.

Professionals such as chaplains, priests, rabbis, and ministers
help people at such critical moments, when they may find their
thoughts paralyzed and their tongues twisted. But even a cardinal found that intense pain made prayer impossible. Joseph
Bernardin wrote:

> *[After surgery] I remember saying to the friends who visited me, 'Pray
> while you're well, because if you wait until you're sick you might not
> be able to do it.' They looked at me, astonished. I said, 'I'm in so much
> discomfort that I can't focus on prayer. My faith is still present. There
> is nothing wrong with my faith but in terms of prayer, I'm just too
> preoccupied with the pain. I'm going to remember that I must pray
> when I am well!'[4]*

His admission is strikingly honest; we who come nowhere near his holiness might well heed his advice, exploring a whole smorgasbord of prayer forms while we still have time, health, and energy.

We may find that in more ordinary circumstances, the trouble with memorized prayers is their monotony. (Please be aware that people who are nourished and sustained by them should keep saying them. Only those who've grown discontented need read further.) We want something that fits a specific situation, or we need a more meaningful language to describe a new experience, or we find the formulas anemic. An analogy might be knowing the Pledge of Allegiance or the Preamble to the Declaration of Independence: good to have stored in the mind somewhere, but hardly the stuff of daily discourse. It's then that we turn to some other possibilities.

SOMETIMES THE LANGUAGE OF PRAYER IS CONVERSATIONAL

To some people, conversation with God comes so easily that they may not think to name it prayer. They punctuate their day with a blessing on a child as they drop her off at school, a call for God's help on a test or a difficult task, a plea for healing a relative who's ill, praise to God for a lovely sunset or a chocolate dessert, a request to find a lost object, thanks to the creator for a friendship or an understanding spouse. In the three examples that follow, you may recognize your own familiar, conversational style.

One woman recounts the story of passing the same house daily on her way to work. The house was dilapidated and needed paint; the same woman always sat by the window. It was hard to see if she was reading, knitting, or simply staring out the window. But the woman who passed regularly was touched, and began a practice of saying, "God bless the lady in the window." She never knew if her blessing had any effect, but she sometimes wonders if someone might be praying for her in the same easy way.

A plumber who encounters many people "near the end of their ropes" counsels, "A prayer, even through clenched teeth, is so much more effective than counting to ten." He may not realize that when he arrives in some homes, *he* is an answer to prayer!

This Dinka prayer from Africa addresses God in simple, conversational tones:

> *Now that the sun has set,*
> *I sit and rest, and think of you.*
> *Give my weary body peace.*
> *Let my legs and arms stop aching.*
> *Let my nose stop sneezing.*
> *Let my head stop thinking.*
> *Let me sleep in your arms.*[2]

SOMETIMES THE LANGUAGE OF PRAYER IS SILENCE

Talking to one other person doesn't require the tactics we use when we speak to a hundred. It's not that hard to get God's attention. Think of it as running into the arms of someone we love. Usually our words at such a moment aren't profound. Even a heartfelt "I missed you" or "It's good to be home" is usually muffled in someone's shoulder. The important thing is the proximity, the feel of a tweed jacket, a soft sweatshirt, or a silky cheek. We breathe deep of that person's familiar smell—newborns, it's said, can recognize their mothers by smell; dogs are adept at it, and adults recognize a particular perfume, hand lotion, or aftershave, a distinctive whiff of garlic. We may even lose track of a conversation's content as we sink into the pleasure of a familiar voice. In short, there's far more to being in someone's presence than words alone. Perhaps an ultimate proof of friendship is that we are able to be together without saying a word.

At times, we simply want to sit with God, saying little or nothing. God must welcome such moments—especially with people who are usually driven by the agenda, the schedule, the calendar. Ah—at last we've stopped to consider what makes it all worthwhile, who makes it all possible. Our reluctance to do nothing seems odd when we consider that it's usually at such times we do everything. A book or a prepared script seems irrelevant then; their absence allows wordlessness to become eloquent.

Thomas Merton once prayed:

To be here with the silence of Sonship in my heart is to be a center in which all things converge upon you. That is surely enough for the time being.

Father, I beg you to keep me in this silence so that I may learn from it the word of your peace and the word of your mercy and the word of your gentleness to the world: and that through me perhaps your word of peace may make itself heard where it has not been possible for anyone to hear it for a long time. [3]

Touch can also be a silent language, if we are sensitized to the many ways God and other people touch us daily. A hug, a well-wrought poem, a hand on the shoulder, a turn of events, a friend's joke, a change in plans—all can be read as God's direct interventions if we're only present to them and respond to God with a simple "Thanks" or "Why?" or "What are you trying to tell me here?"

SOMETIMES THE LANGUAGE OF PRAYER IS TEARS

Tears come when words reach a mysterious boundary marker. The verbal can no longer capture the emotion. We can do no more, say no more; we can only grieve. Like children, we burst into tears almost as an admission of how small we are, how little we can do, how much we need help. "I've reached my limit, God" is the unspoken message. "Now you must take over."

And God who himself wept must respond. "Jesus wept" is the shortest passage in Scripture, and perhaps the most poignant. It occurs outside the tomb of Lazarus, his friend, where Jesus weeps with Lazarus's sisters, Martha and Mary. If Jesus' tears speak loudly, so do ours. God answers with the tenderness of a lover or a parent: the book of Revelation includes the apocalyptic vision of God wiping all the tears from human eyes, when "there will be no more death, and no more mourning or sadness" (Revelation 21:4).

The newly bereaved parent or spouse, the friend or brother or sister grieving in mute anguish must wrench the heart of God as does no other sight. That anyone mourns is proof that

he or she has risked, become vulnerable, given a heart away—
in short, has loved as God has asked. When his wife lay dying,
C. S. Lewis reflected on loss:

> *Without exception, every single person in the world would know at some
> time the excruciating pain of loss. For some . . . it would come from los-
> ing a loved one; for others, it would be having nobody to love. And Jack
> suspected that, by far and away, the first might be easier to bear.*[4]

It is poignant to note that the coming of Jesus into this
world was marked not only by angel song but also by "wailing
and loud lamentation" (Matthew 2:18). The grief of mothers
whose children were slaughtered by Herod echoes the
prophecy of Jeremiah:

> *It was Rachel weeping for her children,*
> *refusing to be comforted*
> *because they were no more.*

Among Jesus' first words to Mary after his resurrection were,
"Woman, why do you weep?" He does not trumpet his own vic-
tory; he focuses on her sorrow. This is not a God who recoils
from the sight of tears, but who spends his life in close proximity to those who weep. Indeed, one of the most touching names
for the Deity is "God who weeps with us."

SOMETIMES THE LANGUAGE
OF PRAYER IS SONG

American advertisers know how an annoying ditty can lodge
itself in the memory and repeat itself incessantly. The executive

en route to a meeting where billions of dollars will change hands may well be humming about hamburgers. At times when we want to be serious, we can't resist the lyrics popping into our heads for "A Book Report on Peter Rabbit," "Twist and Shout," or "It's a Beautiful Day in the Neighborhood." (Author and publisher disclaim responsibility if readers are now stuck with any of those for the remainder of the day. In other words, don't call me if you're trying to remember the refrain for toilet-bowl cleaner.)

Advertisers' success underscores the ways music weaves its way around the psyche. Catholics often joke that "no one leaves church humming the homily," and it's true: one strong line from a hymn may affect our behavior more than any appeal to reason. In 1997, the East Coast Conference for Religious Education celebrated its twenty-fifth anniversary in Washington, D.C. Without hesitation, hundreds of people, led by musician David Haas, belted out songs laden with nostalgia. How many could have recited a book they read or a sermon they heard in 1972?

Some of the liveliest prayer in the Bible is musical: lyre and trumpet, timbrel and castanet all praise the Lord. A group singing together has a unique power: despite the fact that a few are off-key, a few are shrill, and a few bellow, we're expressing a shared belief. And by gum, that makes the quality of our singing secondary. The pros may frown, but sometimes praising God in chorus brings as much joy as a degree from Juilliard.

When we don't take our opportunities for song, the silence is stifling. Perhaps the second most poignant line in Scripture is Jesus' lament for his generation:

They are like children sitting in the marketplace and calling to one
another, 'We played the flute for you and you did not dance; we
wailed, and you did not mourn.' (Matthew 11:17)

How sad if the dance of life should go on without us, if we
don't get caught up in the music, if we fail in the most natural
response to God's song.

Prayer, then, extends to a wide variety of languages. God
knows and can interpret every tongue; we can learn to be more
fluent in the languages of prayer. Formulas, conversations,
silences, tears, and song all join in the chorus. And how many
other languages of prayer, not even named here, also communicate with God?

REFLECT

Complete this sentence: Sometimes the language of prayer is . . .

PRAY

Try praying in a language other than words.

11

SENSE APPEAL

Metaphors for

Prayer

All our bodies want, ever, is to love beauty.

—GERRY GRAHAM

Even for articulate people, words can strain and grind to a halt. When we are overcome with emotion or exhaustion, words fail. It is then that we turn to images, and we discover as many metaphors for prayer as there are people who pray. Some are simple, like carrying before us the face of a friend who is undergoing surgery. Through the day's meetings and traffic jams, meals and phone calls, it may be impossible to voice specific prayers. But the visual image flashes before the mind's eye, and we hold that friend to God, asking for healing.

Among the comparisons that follow, some will appeal; others will fall flat. The ultimate hope is that these images will encourage praying with all the senses. Why should we restrict ourselves to words when God has given us vision, hearing, taste, smell, and touch? Prayer is like . . .

HIKING THROUGH THE FOOTHILLS

Where we walk matters less than *who* we walk with, especially when we walk deliberately with God. This particular hike is not for exercise, or even for scenery, but for listening. We set out with no agenda, perhaps asking only, "What am I looking for, O God?" or "Where are you?"

What makes the foothills especially symbolic terrain is that they mirror in the external world what is happening internally. As when we stroll along the shore, we skirt a large presence. We hover on the fringes of a great mystery like the woman who dared to touch only the hem of Jesus' garment. But we also know that when we are surrounded by so much beauty, we must be close to God.

The mountains on the horizon contain all the colors of twilight, a purple deep as the darkest lilac or iris, blue as the wave's coil. Piled like a sloppy torte, layers of mountains recede into the distance, suggesting the limitless distances of an infinite God. Beneath our feet, long grasses are burnished like a path to an ancient, sacred shrine. We know instinctively why the mountains have always been the privileged place for the encounter with God. We come to them expecting that presence, and their beauty answers. We are not disappointed.

WALKING UNDER AUTUMN TREES

A bough of buttery yellow leaves arches overhead; fallen leaves crunch on the path beneath. As my friend and I walk through autumn foliage, our conversation is intimate. We brush hands as we go; we bend close to catch each other's words. Then I remember: God is inclined toward us. Is this how it works? God is as close as this friend, as eager to catch my words and reply? Do we walk together in more places than I could imagine? Is God truly the hidden companion made up of nothing but empathy, for whom we all long? Do we dare believe that such good news might be true?

DINING WITH A FRIEND

Coming out of the cold evening, the smell of food wraps us in warmth. It is only the beginning of our nurture. No matter how simple the meal, a friend or relative has prepared it carefully. Plenty of cookbooks extol the way that affection seasons a menu; no need to go into it again here.

But we can say that the shared meal gives us a glimpse of God's careful nurture. That peek comes not only through the food but also through the shared prayer beforehand, the taken-for-granted belief that we who dine at the same table look to the same God for our ultimate sustenance. The jokes and confidences exchanged, the laughter joined, the ideas meshed, the work put on hold—all create a space where we can be our best selves. Nothing pompous about scooping up soup; nothing pretentious about tearing into a tortilla. All facades forgotten, we plunge into God trustingly as we dig into a plate, knowing our hunger, knowing we will be fed.

IMMERSING IN WATER

Many images of water come to mind, because water is an archetypal symbol. Herman Melville began *Moby Dick* by describing humanity's attraction to water. Humans flock to shores: "They must get just as nigh the water as they possibly can without falling in." There is magic in the smallest pool. "Yes," he concludes, "as every one knows, meditation and water are wedded for ever."[1]

Furthermore, water is a symbol central to Christianity. In the third century Tertullian wrote, "We . . . are born in water, nor have we any safety in any other way than by permanently abiding in water."[2] Abiding in water makes us think of wrinkled skin and prunelike fingers, but when we think of prayer as an immersion in God, perhaps we can move off the literal level. Some theologians tell us we live in a cosmic soup of possibility, where all is one and dualisms are outmoded. Such a universe—a vast sea of God's presence—corresponds to prayer. But too much water drowns; let's contain it in three specific forms:

Standing in the Rain

This doesn't mean a dreary cold rain that makes waiting for the bus an exercise in misery. It's more like rain falling on the dust bowl, with wrinkled farmers running outside like little kids to watch the parched earth softening. Or the rain in movies that comes just as the leads are about to kiss, and sends them laughing into the picturesque gazebo (which is never so far away that her mascara runs). When we lift our faces to a welcome rain, we find tangible evidence that grace abounds. Drop after shiny drop, bringing forth fragrance of earth or grass and freshness in women and men, with no apparent end in sight: for limited human beings, rain is an icon of God's limitless love.

Slipping into the Hot Tub

People who pray only when fully clothed should probably skip this one. But often after a stressful day, sliding into a hot tub eases all the pressures that accumulate in the neck and shoulders. We leave behind the arguments, unpaid bills, deadlines, and details. For a few moments, our senses reign supreme. The thinking mind takes a brief vacation while the skin soaks in the warmth and silken texture of water. Conversation is reduced to contented sighs as every muscle relaxes.

Perhaps this is how we stand before God. When we lean intentionally into the divine presence, our worries are set aside. We are the satisfied child resting in the parent's lap, in whom the parent takes delight. There's no need for a lot of chatter; we are happy simply to be.

Hearing the Sound of Water

Experts say this auditory image is as soothing to the psyche as the sound of classical music. The splash of falling water recalls freedom, generosity, and abundance, a sense of eternity that captures the endless fidelity and love of God. Jesus promised to give living water that would bubble up to eternal life. We have only to listen for a few moments to be caught up in this particular song of creation and what it might mean for human life. The psalmist wrote:

> *The voice of Yahweh is upon the waters;*
> *the God of glory thunders upon many waters. (Psalm 29:3)*

The sound may convey that we are cleansed of the day's dust in a constant mercy, that water renews us spiritually just as it flows through the healthy body or cools a fever. It symbolizes that pool of hope that is baptism, the Jordan waters that flowed over Jesus, the living water that brings new life.

LOOKING UP INTO APPLE BLOSSOMS

Once a year, grace takes on specific form and fragrance. Looking at the sky through the branches of a blossoming apple tree restores the sense of what a pleasure it is simply to be alive. White petals are sharply outlined against cobalt blue, the background like matting for art. Some buds are brushed with a pink the shade of skin in a Renoir portrait. The beauty is intensified by the brevity—one April shower or one gust of wind could destroy the fragile scene. Sometimes in prayer we recognize for a moment how precious we are, how vulnerable are those we love. Sometimes we glimpse the beauty of God, as delicate as an apple blossom, as tender.

CRAWLING INTO BED AT NIGHT

Finally the masks are hung up with the suits; the pretenses are abandoned. Pajama-wrapped, we surrender the standing posture of control and dominance; we lie down. Perhaps we are most like children then, and any parent knows how lovable a sleeping child can be, despite whatever damage little Attila the Hun wreaked during the day. Sleeping is an act of trust, leaving the world in God's hands until we bumble forth again.

The simple prayer of John XXIII after a long day of papal duties was, "I'm tired and I'm going to bed. It's your church. Take care of it." How easily he dismissed the notion that he might be indispensable; how humbly he put his cares into God's hands. We might all do well to follow his lead, abandoning our fretting, admitting that maybe, after all, God's in charge.

We use metaphor whenever we want to understand a topic better. The best teachers are those who can draw comparisons between the unfamiliar and the familiar. They know that relating a new concept to something we already understand helps us with astronomy or algebra. The same principle applies to prayer. While this chapter explores a few metaphors, others abound. Prayer is also like dancing, like planting seed, like holding a sobbing child. Each person can explore unlimited possibilities.

REFLECT

Complete this sentence: Prayer is like . . .

PRAY

Begin prayer by choosing one of the metaphors above or by creating your own.

12

CALLUSED HANDS

Working Prayer,

Praying Work

All throughout his public life,
Jesus was referred to by his contemporaries as
"Jesus the carpenter," not "Jesus the rabbi."

—CAROL PERRY

Several examples given in the first chapter of people at prayer were people at work: a nurse, a student, a dancer, a business executive, and an artist. While the choice may surprise some who think that prayer occurs in a separate compartment from work, it is not unusual for work to be a prayerful place. After all, for most people, work consumes at least forty hours a week, fifty weeks of the year. That familiar figure doesn't begin to take into account the labor that starts when we get home from the paid job. The endless rounds of laundry, cooking, house maintenance, car washing, errand running, child chauffeuring, paperwork, and yard work constitute another huge block of hours. We know that a God who longs to be with us would not hide during the major portion of our day. So in this chapter we'll look at how we can pray at work and see our work as prayer.

We'll look for ways to make all our working time prayerful. We'll try to bless our work, to see it and its effects as holy. Maybe it's not the perfect job, the creative outlet we'd like it to be; maybe it doesn't utilize all our talents or fully tap our education. But the steady income provides for us and our families; whatever the task, it directs us beyond self-centeredness to care for others. And, as in every other facet of our experience, God awaits us in our work. Our task is to become more conscious of that fact.

OUR TRADITION'S VIEW OF WORK

The Judeo-Christian ethic has consistently commended work. Paul writes, "You know for yourselves that the work I did earned enough to meet my needs and those of my companions. I did this to show you that this is how we must exert ourselves to support the weak" (Acts 20:34–35). The foundational philosophy of the great Benedictine abbeys balanced like a perfect arch on the two pillars of *orare et laborare,* pray and work. So why do we regard work more often as a necessary drudgery than as a route to God? Maybe around Labor Day we see a few magazine articles or hear a talk praising industry, but for the most part, we look down on our work and regret the fact that we don't have more time to pray. Let's look at some possible origins of such division, then attempt a more holistic outlook.

While some voices in the community chorus have praised work, others have reinforced the "necessary evil" attitude that labor is somehow beneath us. When we read books or hear talks on prayer, they often fail to mention this major part of our lives. Religious writers often seem oddly divorced from bottom-line, paycheck realities, as if they live in the unreal zone of a Jane Austen novel or some television sitcoms where no one ever holds down a job. A short time in such company is pleasant, but after a while we want to scream, "All this conversation is lovely, but when do we get down to business? It's ten o'clock in the morning, and no one plans to accomplish anything today? What's *with* you people? Have you no deadlines? No bills to pay?"

We may be embarrassed to blatantly reveal our workaholic bent and cringe to think that we might really be so Waspish, so production oriented, so profit driven. We hide from the frowns of the spiritual writers who cluck gently, "But it's all about *being.* Work is a lower life-form. We must attain the higher planes of contemplation. Try to reduce your desires for luxuries, and focus on the heavenly good."

Admittedly, that sounds slightly nineteenth century. But we've all heard the well-intentioned sermons, usually prompted by the lilies-of-the-field gospel, when we are told that materialism is the root of evil, and we'd all be much happier if we'd cut back on the consumerism. After which, the homilist drives a car purchased and repaired by someone else, to a dinner cooked and cleaned up by someone else, eaten in a home paid for by someone else. He (yup, in most cases it's a "he") doesn't know the cost of tuition, textbooks, orthodontists, prescriptions, charity drives, and groceries generated by our rabidly materialistic offspring. Ah, how those four-year-olds max out the credit cards!

Meanwhile, the faithful listeners dash home from church and try to squeeze in a sandwich before the (check one) car wash, play practice, birthday party, soccer game, grocery store, committee meeting, nursing-home visit, while the scolding resounds in their ears. "Sure, we're rampant materialists," they'd probably concede. "But when do we have time to think about it?"

How did we come so far from the earthy, hardworking roots of our religion—the Hebrew farmers, vintners, and herders; the fisherfolk, tax collectors, and soldiers who populate the Gospels? At one point in our liturgy, the presider used to wash his hands because they were grubby from the goats, vegetables, and chickens that people brought to the altar. When he raised the offerings, "the fruit of the vine, the work of human hands," people could nod knowingly; they had slivers of dirt lodged in their fingernails and grass stains on their pants. Yet somehow we got caught up in notions of ritual purity—the hands that touched the sacred vessels couldn't be sullied by contact with tractors.

OUR ATTITUDES TOWARD WORK

Now that goats and chickens are rarely seen in church, we tend to idealize the bygone agrarian society, disregarding work done in a high-tech lab, an urban office, or a computerized library. We respect calluses, but not carpal tunnel syndrome. Contemporary work patterns tend to be abstract, specialized, hard for an observer to appreciate.

It's a problem for people who observe the annual "Take Your Daughter to Work" day. Nothing wrong with the goal here: let our daughters observe women in the workplace so they have strong role models with whom to identify and career goals to which they can aspire. But unless the experience is embroidered, it often bores the daughters. They see their parents sitting at computers, attending meetings, talking on the phone, poring over charts or machines or blueprints, but what is in fact hard work does not look dramatic or appealing. Dad doesn't drive triumphantly through the front gate with a wagonload of hay; he simply sits behind a desk. Mom doesn't display her homemade jam at the county fair; she speaks into a headset. It's all rather puzzling to the kiddies.

We share some of their puzzlement if our core images of work hearken back to gleaners in wheat fields, softly lit by the setting sun. Since we don't sweat over crops, we don't regard any work as holy. We create dichotomies: this twenty minutes carved from a busy schedule is prayer. This eight- or ten-hour stretch can't count as prayer because it's work. We yearn to "get away" so we can *really* pray, totally disregarding the fact that the work of nurturing others, using our talents, and contributing what we can to God's reign on earth is itself a mighty prayer.

Perhaps we have too long divorced prayer from action. Mention the word *prayer,* and most people think of a chapel where a solitary figure wrapped in the glow of stained glass kneels or sits in silence. This person may be doing something splendid, but it's not the only form of prayer. While the retreat to a silent, beautiful place heals and refreshes many people, brings a deep and indisputable peace, and should be a regular part of everyone's routine, the retreat center is not the place where most of us live. Perhaps we need to remember that "Jesus knew and was part of the work world; it was his callused hands that gave the healing touch."[1] Where he was, we are.

IN PRAISE OF A
MARKETPLACE SPIRITUALITY

The voices praising work as prayer may be few, but they sound loud and clear. Carol Perry points out that work wasn't a punishment for the sin of Adam and Eve. They tended the garden *before* the fall; work seemed to be part and parcel of the human condition.[2] In our day, one measure of health for someone who's languished with an illness is the cheerful announcement "She's feeling better; she's going back to work tomorrow!" Much as we may complain about work, unemployment brings the kiss of death.

Joan Chittister adds, "Good work that leaves the world softer and fuller and better than ever before is the stuff of which human satisfaction and spiritual value are made. There will come a moment in life when we will have to ask ourselves what we spent our lives on and how life in general was better as a result of it. On that day we will know the sanctifying value of work."[3]

This theory rings true only in application. So let's take the philosophy through an ordinary workday—with the caveat that the experience of one person is never that of another. The example is given as a guideline; each person can fill in the blanks.

PRAYING THROUGH AN ORDINARY WORKDAY

For most people, the day's work doesn't begin in the office; it starts long before they arrive at a paid job. Through the whole string of early morning rituals, we may in fact offer others an easy, unmeditated care that will help them through the day. Signing the child's permission slip for the field trip, pouring the spouse's coffee, finding the missing socks, picking up the car pool, making the salad for the potluck are such routine examples that we take them for granted. But if they don't happen, some wheels grind to a serious halt. If we perform these actions mindfully, we too can see their wide influence. If we pause at some point to analyze what's going on, we can appreciate it: I am doing this from love; I am honoring my commitments; I am fulfilling a role given me by God; I am *being* prayer.

Perhaps on the commuter train or bus, we reflect more deliberately. We read the advice of Thich Nhat Hanh: "You have to practice looking at all living beings with the eyes of compassion."[4] It seems a large order, but the practice can start during the first exchange with the office receptionist. If we remember to ask how her bowling game went last night, it means she is no longer faceless, a functionary who answers the phone and makes the coffee. She is a daughter of God, created in the divine image. Honoring her interests is a step toward a larger compassion.

Dealing with the accumulated mail and messages can be an annoying chore, or it can be done in the spirit of the publisher who once said, "I want to answer every phone call with the conviction that it's Christ on the other end of the line." His ideal can carry over into that staple of modern business, the committee meeting.

Before the meeting, or if possible, earlier in the day, we can meditate on a few principles that make even the dreariest session more prayerful. We can come in an attitude of peace, knowing that our inner state will have some bearing on the outcome. If we insist on bringing our personal gripes, our own agendas, and our desires for ego gratification, that will surely affect the business at hand. If, on the other hand, we vow to disarm our hearts and quiet our ambitions, despite the dispositions of everyone else at the table, the meeting can be for us a more prayerful experience.

And what about relationships with everyone else? If we try to see through eyes of compassion, we enjoy our co-workers' humor, their resilience, their variety of talents. If we come from a place of prayer, we may know more easily when to confront problems and when to let them go. We can be aware of the axiom that the Western mind is incapable of going for ten minutes without a negative thought. Maybe we can push that time span to twelve minutes; maybe we can rest content in not expressing every single criticism.

Perhaps one's work is less social. Maybe it's prolonged contact with car motors or spreadsheets, forms or food. With a few deep breaths, we can be grateful for a body that does our bidding, for limbs that accomplish these tasks, for skills that help us perform. We might think of the people who will ultimately be blessed by our labors: the family able to resume its car trips, the young couple whose loan application has been quickly processed, the small business that will profit from our marketing or accounting expertise, the hungry people who will eat the meal we cooked.

If we attend to our work as God-given and directed, we see in it more possibilities for the sacred. We might give it an extra oomph, bring order into chaos, try different options, ask, How can we do this better, faster, more creatively? Even if we're caught in a Dilbert-style operation, we can still define our parameters and, no matter how low the boss's IQ, do work in which we take pride.

We need to not only see our work as prayer; we need prayer to infuse our work. The lively spark of grace can show us alternative approaches when ours fail to solve a problem; help us slog through work that is drudgery; give impetus when we tire; show us another way, a brighter side, a human dimension veiled before. Sometimes it brings buoyancy, detours, motivation, breakthroughs, helpful companions. Always it reminds us that God is with us, no matter how frustrated we may become.

As the day winds down or the shift ends, many of us need a chocolate, a cup of coffee, a second wind, an infusion of energy—or a prayer. In the late afternoon, some people close the office door and take a two-minute rest to remember they are God's daughters and sons. Some use the ringing of the phone as a call to holiness—taking the moment before answering or the moment after as a time to turn thoughts to God.

The commute home can also be the opportunity for a prayerful transition. What if, instead of cursing traffic, we used the time to thank God for the day's surprises, for projects accomplished, for the energy that made the work possible?

What if we identified the times we felt most distant from God as well as the moments of presence? What if we revisited the laughter, the insights, the deadlines met, and savored those achievements? Instead of cataloguing what to do when we get home or listing tomorrow's jobs, let's review today's work. Let's see ourselves as co-creators, people specifically gifted and missioned by God. Then we might arrive home in a better mood, seeing that the worlds of work and home, labor and leisure aren't separated by a huge gulf. We can bless both places as holy ground.

REFLECT

Have you thought much about your work as prayer? What new insights do you gain from approaching work this way? What difficulties do you have with this approach? ◆ Think through an ordinary workday. What activities do you find most prayerful? least prayerful?

PRAY

My work praises God by . . . ◆ My work serves others by . . . ◆ My work expands me by . . .

13

THANK GOD!

A Grateful Prayer

When you arise in the morning,
give thanks for the morning light,
for your life and strength.
Give thanks for your food
and the joy of living.

If you see no reason for giving thanks,
the fault lies in yourself.

—TECUMSEH

Sometimes I imagine a conversation with my Irish great-great-grandmother. She says in disbelief, "What? You have hot water all the time, whenever you want, inside your house? You work *indoors*? All your children have shoes—and you don't worry about what they will eat? There's always enough food, even in early spring?" She tries to remain cordial, but a stern look creeps across her face. "Aye, darlin'! Whatever could you be *complainin'* about?"

Whatever our particular ancestry, we in the U.S. could imagine similar conversations. Like the Irish who arrived here in coffin ships and the Africans in slave ships, almost every immigrant group faced hardship, poverty, and discrimination during their early years in this country. Any hope for the future must have been smothered by oppression, exhausted by the sheer struggle to survive.

One of the hardest things for any parent must have been watching their children die. That slow, painful process as the limbs went flaccid, the energy ebbed, and the bright cheeks faded must have tortured parents who blamed themselves for not providing the necessary food or medicine. Even for the wealthy, the quick cure of penicillin or another drug, so readily available today, was totally undreamed of.

We take for granted our central heat or air-conditioning, our easy access to education, travel, clothing, and entertainment. But a little reading of history can be sobering. We who recite Psalm 23 in a carpeted church cannot begin to imagine what it must have meant to slaves who clung to that green meadow, sure path, and overflowing cup. For a people in bondage, the story, the world of imagination created a better world than the one in which they lived. That Psalm offered them hope and survival. Do we see it as such a lifeline?

Not to oversimplify: praying from a different context does not make prayer any less meaningful or real. We may not struggle with starvation, but we still contend with illness, stress of every sort, difficult relationships, financial problems, and a host of complexities created by the electronic age. Despite our creature comforts, we are an anxiety-prone people. When we bring our problems to prayer, as we must, they may have different names and faces, but they are no less real than our ancestors' concerns.

GRATITUDE: A MISSING THEME

One theme that should sound noisily and frequently in our prayer is too often lacking. We constantly petition: for health, a better job, a change of heart in someone we love, success in some area. But how often do we thank? Pure, simple gratitude, uncluttered by further requests—does it enter our prayer often enough? Or are we so bent on attaining more that we don't appreciate what we've got?

Perhaps the whininess of the eighties has changed its tone; as we grow older, we learn to put gratitude into the inner space once occupied by greed. A best-selling book offers white space and lines on which people record five things a day for which they are grateful. While it's a step in the right direction, do we really need to buy the book? Can't the attitude enfold our hearts? For if we are not grateful, how can we expect our children to learn the art? If we focus only on acquiring more, why are we surprised when they are demanding?

We who are concerned not only about how gratefully we live, but also about how we affect future generations, might look to a similar situation. When St. Benedict wrote a rule for his followers (incidentally, one that would endure for fifteen hundred years), we might have expected him to be concerned about morality, purpose, and organization. How to whip these barbarians into shape? Surely, give them hefty penances and abundant self-denial; then toss in a few dire threats!

Instead, he is refreshingly unpredictable, focusing on gratitude:

The first rule is simply this:

live this life
and do whatever is done,
in a spirit of Thanksgiving.

Abandon attempts to achieve security,
they are futile,

give up the search for wealth,
it is demeaning,

quit the search for salvation,
it is selfish,

and come to comfortable rest
in the certainty that those who
participate in this life
with an attitude of Thanksgiving
will receive its full promise. [1]

A PERSONAL LIST OF THANKS

For what shall we be grateful? Reading *Roots, Rain of Gold, The Joy Luck Club,* or *Angela's Ashes* attunes us to the struggles of our ancestors, and leaves us grateful that we no longer fight certain battles because they won them for us. Any vivid history book can give us the flavor of life before refrigeration, social welfare, civil rights, painkillers, public education, and jet travel. A few minutes thinking about the absence of any one of the luxuries we take for granted should send us singing into the courts of praise.

Then we may turn more directly to personal blessings. For the climber and student portrayed in chapter 1, gratitude welled from experience. Both were exhausted, but the first offered wordless praise for the beauty of a mountain vista, and the second breathed gratitude for God's help in accomplishing all he had to do that day. For what can we give thanks?

- the pleasant surprises of one day

- good health

- friendships, family, other nurturing relationships

- the help given by our religious traditions: the community, Scripture, sacraments, art and music, leaders, inspiration

- homes and jobs

- food and clothing

- natural beauty

- the freedoms protected by the Constitution

This list is only a beginning. Answering the following questions prayerfully can also encourage gratitude.

What combination of factors has placed us where we are, and how can we see the divine hand there? Sometimes even painful events directed us into what turned out to be a better relationship, career, or living situation.

How many insignificant details come together to make a day flow more smoothly, or to help us accomplish what we're about? Are we grateful for these? To people who have endured a series of car repairs, the hum of a smooth ignition sounds like music— do we remember to say thanks for such a routine event?

Anyone who's had the slightest brush with a hospital is grateful for health—do we appreciate the functioning of our respiratory, digestive, and reproductive systems?

If we visualize our days like patchwork, a whole crazy quilt of events and people and places coming together in a unique way, then thanks might stitch it all together. Was it happenstance or blessing to find that lost form, be delayed by traffic, or take that phone call? While we may come to thanks through the back door, other experiences can usher us directly into thanks. A recent confluence of events shows how even a slow study like me, caught by surprise, can breathe thanks like a psalmist.

PSALM OF PRAISE

I had preceded a business trip to Los Angeles with an overnight stay in San Diego, knowing that a day by the ocean was well worth the expense of a rental car and the hassles with traffic that the detour would entail. Despite a long siege of coastal storms the previous week, that day was clear. The waves crashed high and fierce on the shore; as they buckled, the sequins of sunlight caught in the curl. Shimmering and roaring along a broad, magnificent beach, the ocean displayed a natural power at once humbling and exhilarating. Anyone who wouldn't be caught up in such grandeur and filled with gratitude must be numb, totally blind to beauty.

I breathed my puny thanks and, perhaps more importantly, sank deeply into the scene. I slept with the rhythms of waves in my dreams, woke to the sea's majesty oscillating in the early morning fog, walked miles along the polished surfaces of its shores. For a day I was immersed in ocean world, grateful for every sparkle and glint of myriad lights on infinite waters.

Such an experience of abundance must have lain behind Dom Helder Camara's prayer:

> *May your bounty teach me*
> *greatness of heart.*
> *May your magnificence*
> *stop me being mean.*
> *Seeing you a prodigal*
> *and open-handed giver*
> *let me give unstintingly*
> *like a king's [child]*
> *like God's own.*[2]

Filled with gratitude, we can act more nobly, behave more often as if we were descended from royal lineage, daughters and sons of God.

My own gratitude took on a human dimension the next day. During a lovely dinner with close friends, I felt a similar wave of affirmation and support. Good food and good company are a rare combination that surpass any wording afterward on the "thanks for your hospitality" cards. My three dinner companions were some of the people I most admire; our conversation spilled over with humor and lingered on topics that fascinated us all. So much goodness concentrated around one table: everyone should, at least once in a lifetime, dine in such abundance.

My friends' compliments to my work will keep me going for a long time; I sailed back to my hotel room on a tide of Chardonnay and gratitude. In one respect, the two experiences of ocean and dinner weren't that different; both overwhelmed with lavish abundance. My response to both was similar: like a child tearing open gifts on her birthday, I wanted to repeat "thank you thank you thank you."

I suspect that if each of us mined our experience, we could unearth one day or one hour that glimmers in the memory like treasure. The elderly seem to turn those jewels over and over in the mind as they would in the palm of their hands. Savoring our memories need not lead to idealizing the past; rather, it may better alert us to the joys of the present.

THE MODEL OF JESUS

We know how much it means to be thanked for something we have done, and how it rankles when our efforts seem to be overlooked. God doesn't seethe with bitter reproach, but Jesus, the human face of God, grinned with delight when one leper returned to thank him for a cure. "Where are the other nine?" he asked in surprise. How embarrassingly often we count ourselves with those nine. How much more often we could turn to praise like number ten.

Henri Nouwen wrote, "Gratitude is not an obvious attitude toward life but must be deliberately chosen in the face of all the evidence that pulls us toward bitterness and despair."[3] We have in Jesus a model of one who, knowing that the passion and cross awaited him, nevertheless joined his friends in a circle of comradeship and praise, giving thanks for bread almost in defiance of the ordeal that would follow. His last supper, his last gift direct us to repeat one word in our lives: thanks.

REFLECT

Unearth one day or one hour that gleams in your memory like treasure. Savor it.

PRAY

Even on a deadening day, when I am ill or tired, I can find one thing for which to be grateful. Today I am most grateful for . . .

14

TRANSFORMING TIME

A Liturgy of the Hours

The lands of sunrise and sunset
you fill with your joy.

—PSALM 65:8

A regular marking of time by prayer is one way to transform time. This is one goal of people who punctuate the day with the Divine Office, or Liturgy of the Hours. Nothing, they believe, matches the importance of continually praising God. Humans are made to praise and thank the creator. So at regular intervals, they drop what they are doing and sing or recite Psalms and prayers specific to the hour.

While the practice seems uniquely suited to monks and nuns in monasteries or convents, it is regaining popularity among laypeople. Not that they halt a business meeting or quit feeding the baby to say Sext (the midday prayer); they adapt the Divine Office to their schedules in a variety of ways. They create adaptations because they like the ancient poetry, the sense of order, the rhythm it can bring to days that might otherwise seem fragmented, diffuse, or cluttered.

These advocates learn to overlook some of the mind-boggling directives found in older guidebooks, where fusty authors fretted "if several celebrations should occur on the same day." (Clearly these monastics were never parents contending with one kid's birthday, another's field trip, and a third's piano recital!) Just as some people blip over the names in Russian novels, so we can treat the Liturgy of the Hours with some liberality. Most folks are better off ignoring the excruciating detail about which verse to say on which solemnity, and simply going with the general flow.

The idea of praying around the clock is so appealing that we might try adapting the idea, substituting spontaneous prayer for the Psalms and readings formally assigned to the hours of the day. Such adaptation is in keeping with a general principle: if prayer forms appeal, don't let them collect dust. Better to make them practical than to forget them completely. Just as the stuff of one person's life is woven into the examples that follow, so anyone can bring personal experience into the general framework.

To expand on this technique, the following meditations are loosely based on the traditional hours of Lauds (morning), Sext (noon), None (afternoon), Vespers (evening), and Matins (immediately after midnight). The reflections are based on the Psalms traditionally used at these times of day. Liturgical purists may be appalled at the free adaptation, but they might agree that praying the Divine Office even in casual form is preferable to not praying it at all.

MORNING PRAYER: SKI SLOPE

I have always loved the clear purity of morning prayer, the best time of the day given to God before the frustrations mount, the obligations accumulate, and the details wind me into knots. At home, after everyone has left for the day, I can have a second cup of coffee with God.

That didn't work on a day when I surrendered the silence for a rowdy ski trip with eight teenagers. As one friend kindly pointed out, the adventure held the potential for thirty-six broken limbs. The alarm beeped early, starting a crazy circus of feeding everyone donuts and juice, packing luggage and ski gear, checking out of the hotel, and driving the whole crew to the ski area. It was hardly a time of pristine stillness, monastic bells echoing through the quiet.

But somehow, miraculously, I hadn't yet missed morning prayer. God must have a special compassion for the chaperones of large, young flocks. After all had visited the bathroom, bought lift tickets, and skied off to slopes for varying ability levels, I was alone on the mountain, my twelve-year-old daughter a cozy companion. It was too early for vast crowds; as I followed her down the mountain, our tracks were undisturbed. Together, we had the great privilege of entering into God's beauty and abundance. Our trails down the mountain made a perfect series of *S*s.

All around us reared up mountains. Waves of blue, gray, and white granite splashed over each other and lapped the sky. Crisp air was lightly scented with pine. The snow was lavish and deep, satin in texture. As with any physical activity, I ski better when I don't think about it. Over the years I've learned to hum or whistle some simple melody to establish a rhythm. When my turns fit the tempo, it frees my mind to wander, to admire the surroundings.

Or in this case, to pray. What I did on that mountain didn't fit the monastic tradition of prayer—long, isolated stretches in a hushed chapel. It came closer to the Ignatian ideal of "finding God in all things." But because this way is relatively new to most of us, we make the path by walking (or in this case, by skiing). The hymn "Give Me Only Your Love and Your Grace" fit perfectly into turns. "Take Lord" (right turn), "Receive" (left). "Your Love" (right) and "Your Grace" (left). It was as if lightly, with a silken swish, I moved from one careful palm of God's hand to the other.

I know that God goes with us everywhere, and that always I am in those tender hands. Only once in a great while, though, do I have an opportunity to visualize such security. That glimpse is not confined to Colorado; it can come on Atlantic or Pacific beaches, in the soft hills of Pennsylvania, along the gleaming shores of the Great Lakes, or in the lush gardens of North Carolina. Wherever we pause to appreciate God's creation, there we find serenity and lavish generosity.

Not that I had left all my worries in the city. One nagging anxiety stood out in bold relief against this setting. The previous week, my friend Judy had been diagnosed with terminal cancer. Skiing made me think of her because we had gone so often together—at first, with a flock of our kids. Later, we discovered the thrill of adult company, two or three women on a Saturday adventure.

A native of the Rocky Mountain region, Judy had skied since high school. In contrast to this Missouri klutz who had learned the sport late in life, she skied with poise and speed. I remember following her graceful turns, the powdery puffs behind her skis, as if I were watching ballet. Her lavender jacket fluttered like a moth, shadowing the snow. She was always ahead of me, but she'd always wait for me to catch up, never criticize my slowness.

So a ski slope was the perfect place for me to struggle with her diagnosis. Each time I hear devastating news, I wrestle with an attempt to bring the lens of faith to bear on it. There on the run we had skied together, I prayed that Judy might have the peace of the white corridor between the green pines, the grace of easy turns. She will be ahead of me again now, on another path, but I asked that she meet there the warm welcome of friends around the fire. May her last run be long, with a heavenly hot tub at the end.

That day the trails' names became almost a litany: Prelude, Rhapsody, Soliloquy, Windsong, Copperfield, Jacques Pique,

Alleluia. By the time we skied the Four O'Clock Run to the car, the clouds had caught the sunset like a fine golden mesh. I remembered then how Christ seeks always to catch us in the net of his compassion. Ever teacher and artist, he provides us with all the tactile, visual reminders we need. Always and everywhere, he reigns over our lives, even on a ski slope—especially there.

NOON THIRST: BILLOWS AND BREAKERS

Water images fill Psalm 42: the deer longing for running waters, the soul thirsting for God, the deep calling unto deep. Do these metaphors appeal only to those who live in deserts, or for whom it is a constant battle to secure fresh water? Can we who so easily turn the tap ever appreciate what that scarcity must have meant? When we're hot and dusty, we take a shower. We carry insulated water bottles when we hike, run, or exercise. The washing machine hums cozily alongside the dishwasher—appliances we take for granted until that rare occasion when they break down. Then we may agonize, but only until the repair truck arrives. Are we spoiled, then, so rich in water that the ancient symbol fails to speak?

I think not. I think that in some ways we thirst even more starkly than the ancients. In our day, thirst may take the form of loneliness, disillusionment, stress, insecurity, a longing for clarity or certainty, agonizing over other people, an unsettling suspicion that there are no hard-and-fast answers to anything. At this level beyond the physical, we long for the same thing, the only surety, the face of God. We could pray with Catherine of Siena:

You are a mystery as deep as the sea; the more I search, the more I find, and the more I find the more I search for you. But I can never be satisfied; what I receive will ever leave me desiring more. When you fill my soul I have an even greater hunger, and I grow more famished for your light. I desire above all to see you, the true light, as you really are.[1]

It's all a human being wants, really. Not laws and restrictions. Not reminders of past failures. Not impossible expectations. Nothing much different from what people wanted when they followed Jesus to the Judean hills. Or what Catherine asked: "Eternal Trinity, Godhead, mystery deep as the sea, you could give me no greater gift than the gift of yourself."[2]

Sometimes people receive what they seek. The psalmist remembers times of happy procession, "with glad shouts and songs of thanksgiving, a multitude keeping festival" (42:4). We too can remember times when our hearts were light and our companions close. We gathered for some event—a ritual perhaps, or a dance, a wedding, or a long-awaited feast. There were friends, music, flowers, flags, laughter, banners, food, and drink. We drew together and didn't want to leave. All the arduous planning and preparatory work were worth it, tossed like offerings into the glad bonfire of forgotten time.

We may think those events are too rare, yet part of what makes them special is their infrequency. Their momentum keeps us going for a long time—Christmas memories warm us in February; Fourth of July fireworks echo in the explosions of autumn colors. So, if we have brief glimpses of God's face, it sensitizes us to seek more. Knowing that God is not stingy, we start looking for those hints in our most boring routines, our most heavily scheduled hours. As the psalmist says, "By day the

Lord commands his steadfast love, and at night his song is
with me" (42:8).

Lest we ever dismiss the psalmist as a delusional author who
whistles (ever so skillfully) in the dark, we should note the
Psalms' famous dramatic reversals, 360-degree pivots that only
God's grace could cause. The soul that is downcast, mourning,
oppressed, and mocked, knows the remedy and seeks again that
face: "So will I remember you." God comes in a return of water
imagery: the roar of cataracts, the waves of the sea. When words
fail, the image is an adept way to suggest the divine abundance:
"All your waves and your billows have gone over me" (42:7).

Anyone who has plunged into the ocean knows the feeling
of being a tiny piece of driftwood caught up in a powerful
force. We swallow salt water; we lose our footing, tumble and
float. After a crazy somersault through seaweed, we laugh and
do it again. In retrospect, we might call such an experience a
restorer of perspective. It's a potent reminder that there are cosmic plans and divine designs far greater than our particular
griefs or current irritations. Perhaps when we glimpse God's
face, it is at once more vast and more intimate than we could
ever imagine. And more compelling—drawing us so intently
that we spend our lives searching for another glimpse.

AFTERNOON: WATERED GARDEN

Someone has said that "summer afternoon" is the loveliest
phrase in the English language. The month of June is a psalm
itself, a perfect song of praise. Heavy with blossom, flowering
boughs bend over paths; petals pale as shells cover the lawn.
Before the intense summer heat, columbine and dianthus still
bloom; lobelia trails its deep blue train. Roses unfurl their per-

fect pastel cones. It is a feast for the sense of smell; white clusters on an anonymous bush float fragrance on the air.

Perhaps we could not appreciate June if we had not come to it on wintry paths. Part of its joy is the ease of slipping outside without the encumbrance of winter coats. Like amphibians who span two worlds, we live both indoors and outdoors now—with as much of the latter as possible. We appreciate the garden's thriving life more because we have seen it in dull, camel tones: its branches bare, its colors muted.

How appropriate that the garden metaphor, both Eden and the place of Mary Magdalene's encounter with the gardener/risen Jesus, should be so central to the Christian experience. Long after the agendas have curled like papyrus and the schemes have faded, after the Tudors and the Stuarts and the Bourbons had their day, through all the ups and downs, wars and insurrections, the gardens continue. Their flowering and freezing are a seasonal reminder both of life's brevity and of what endures.

Sometimes when we're fortunate, our personal dramas play against such a background. After a drive through the desert we came one afternoon into the oasis of San Diego, its great bodies of water shimmering in the sun like beacons to those who have crossed a dead zone. At a hacienda in Old Town, courtyards were filled with fountains and flowers; the bougainvillea cascaded down the white stucco walls in an avalanche of fuchsia. From the wooden balcony, we could hear the splash of water on stone below—a sound made more welcome by our thirst earlier that afternoon. Red-tiled Spanish roofs shaded the patios, where people sat beneath umbrellas sipping cool drinks. The scent of jasmine wafted on the evening breeze. The calendar may have said February, but to our spirits, that trip brought the summer.

To such scenes of bounty and abundance, God compares us. "Their life shall become like a watered garden, and they shall never languish again" (Jeremiah 31:12). The bouquet of June, the garden after the desert, the smell of earth during rain: we are like these. Our work brings forth beauty and fruit; we are not only hired gardeners but the garden itself, pure gift. We may endure wintry seasons, but unbounded joy is our ultimate inheritance.

How can we so confidently claim such blessing? Will all the dry and joyless paths of our lives lead into these soothing oases of color, texture, and sound? For answer, we have the promise. For reassurance, we turn to the source: "For with you is the fountain of life; in your light we see light" (Psalm 36:9).

EVENING PRAYER: SUNSET

I had arrived at the retreat house in time for an evening Mass. The homily on doorways, windows, and thresholds sensitized me to the wonders of borderlands. The homilist was an excellent photographer who illustrated his talk with pictures of these zones of demarcation—indoors and outdoors, land and sea, day and night, horizon and sky. While seeding those images, he spoke of Jesus, the face of divine and human intersection. After Moses saw God, he wore a veil to modify the glow on his face, too brilliant for human sight. How then do we look upon the face of Christ? I carried the question into the evening.

Many different people show me different faces of Jesus. The survivor of a stroke, his hands gnarled, his spine bent, speaks of the risen Lord, and his crooked posture gives ironic weight to his argument. My rowdy, disrespectful friend who gleefully sends outrageous greeting cards hasn't missed my birthday in thirty years—such funny camouflage for such deep care. Two religious sisters belong to the same order, yet one is the essence of tranquility. She creates for me a safe harbor, her soft voice soothing my fiercest anxiety. The other is an off-the-scale extravert; when she eats at a restaurant, she engages in lively conversation with every waitress. She launches me beyond my natural introversion—flags flying, whistles tooting, band playing.

So it is with thoughts of different worlds meeting that I watch the sunset. In the kind of coincidence that we have come to recognize as God's hand at play, this one is spectacular. At first, long fingers of clear light reach through the clouds. Then the curtains begin to part; the clouds frame rosy patches beyond. My head swims with metaphor: Is the night closing a last casement on the day? What real or symbolic windows are opening onto the transcendent? The sky is dimpled with pink twists, as though the light could be caught in a cord of clouds. Spicy orange and passionate magenta silhouette the purple hills in a color combination only the most deranged pyrotechnist would attempt.

As though to bring me back to earth, two deer stroll by nonchalantly, oblivious to the sunset, more interested in grazing the tawny grasses. Their delicate steps, unlike my fumbling verbiage, give perfect praise to the grains of the earth and the valleys decked with wheat. At one level, I have understood the psalmist's lines:

> You provide for the earth;
> you drench its furrows,
> you level it, soften it with showers,
> you bless its growth. (65:11)

I've seen muddy fields, have even accumulated softened earth on my hiking boots. But I'd never thought of *mountains* softening. Their granite profiles have defined the horizon for centuries—how could such solid boulders shift? Then I saw the phenomenon called *alpenglow*—whole rock faces gilded pink in the sun's last rays.

The soft tones we associate with snug nurseries and baby blankets cover the remotest alpine peaks. In the transitional times of day, our clearest certitudes modulate; our most avid stances relax. We let go of the day's business and turn our faculties over to delight. Perhaps this was what the psalmist meant by

> *The hills are girded with joy . . .*
> *They shout for joy, yes, they sing.* (65:13)

In the wild abandon of God's creation, color can sing, and birdsong can texture the mountainside.

NIGHT: LESSONS IN SLEEP

While the ancients prayed for deliverance from sloth, we moderns might take the opposite tack. Compulsive about work, filled with worry, we must learn to sleep. We may lie down on firm mattresses with percale sheets, but in the psyche, prickly question marks still poke and prod; anxieties lurking deeper than the conscious level nudge us awake. How often do we climb into bed listing what we *didn't* accomplish today? How nervously do we run through tomorrow's agenda, ticking off either our preparations or lack of them? How frequently do we jump out of bed to check on the essential notes for the talk, find the shirt that must match the rest of the outfit, tuck the report into the briefcase?

How ironic that we cannot learn a skill mastered by toddlers. Thumbs planted firmly in mouths, our children drop heavily and deliciously into what the carol "O Little Town of Bethlehem" calls a "deep and dreamless sleep." We, on the other hand, toss and turn and revisit each conversation, each twist in the day's plot, each nuance of every decision. Now it is history, but we continue to rehash. To make matters worse, we anticipate the next day, planning what we'll do and say in detail so elaborate it could never materialize. Then we compound the irony: How will we ever get through the overloaded day ahead on such a paralyzing lack of sleep?

The ancients who prayed for salvation from roaring beasts and lions could have been describing our night demons, our noisy inner voices. They found relief in trust:

On my bed I will remember you,
and through the night watches I will meditate on you. (Psalm 63:6)

To whom do we turn for comfort? Our models may not be helpful at 3 A.M., but like stars, they bless our sleepless nights. The psalmist counsels:

It is vain that you rise up early
and go late to rest,
eating the bread of anxious toil;
for [the Lord] gives sleep to his beloved. (Psalm 127:2)

So much for workaholism: ironically, God's gifts come when we do not grab them, but when we snooze innocently.

Examples of this tranquility extend from Jesus' time to ours. Joseph was surely as anxiety ridden as any unmarried father and probably endured a few sleepless nights himself. Yet Matthew twice records an angel visiting him during a dream (1:20 and 2:13), a good sign that sometimes Joseph slept.

Jesus could be placed into the category of "gifted sleeper"; in a boat during a raging storm, he remained "asleep on the cushion" (Mark 4:38). Following his shining example, Peter managed to sleep in prison, while fastened with double chains—how comfy! (Acts 12:6).

And what of us? Often a rare grace comes after a sleepless night or two. We recognize the warning signs in ourselves: crankiness, headachy fog, slowness in making decisions. We go to bed early, and if we are lucky, we have a warm conversation, a good book, or the sound of rain to tuck us in. Sometimes a sympathetic child, friend, or spouse will say, "You look bushed. I'll clean up the kitchen." Carried on the tide of such blessing, we surrender our troubles with a phrase of Psalm 36: "Leave it to the Lord." Unresolved dilemmas lose their power to torment as we sink into a long and self-forgetting oblivion. Fatigue covers us like a quilt. Like the writer of Psalm 131, we know firsthand:

It is enough for me to keep my soul still and quiet,
like a child in its mother's arms. (2)

We have rested content in God's arms. Now we can rise refreshed to meet the gifts and burdens unique to this day:

There may be tears during the night,
but joy comes in the morning. (Psalm 30:5)

Those who awaken from a good deep sleep know how uniquely sweet it can be. Energy restored, we give thanks for a new day, its potential fresh before us. For eight hours, we let go of everything and, in the process, learn how little we need.

We could say our night prayer to Jesus, lying tranquilly in a rocking boat with his head on a pillow as storms raged about him. "You are our peace, our rest. Someday we will slip into the long sleep of eternity. For now, let us sleep securely in you."

REFLECT

Have you ever tried to punctuate the day with prayer? How did it go? ◆ Choose a Psalm and expand an experience of morning, noon, afternoon, evening, or night into a meditation.

PRAY

Going to bed at night, pray Psalm 4:8: "As soon as I lie down I peacefully go to sleep; / you alone, my strength, keep me perfectly safe." ◆ Awakening, pray Psalm 5:3: "In the morning you hear my voice; / at dawn I will make ready and watch for you."

15

JOURNEY TO JERUSALEM

The Prayer of Imagination

*Here sleeps the blessed Chione, who has found
Jerusalem for she prayed much.*
—FOURTH-CENTURY EPITAPH, ASIA MINOR

Chione probably never left her village. She carved ruts in the path during her daily trudge to the well and grew tired of pettiness, routine, gossip, and a small-town narrowness more stifling than any of us in cyberspace could imagine. Yet she had been to Jerusalem, marveled at its stone towers and lofty pinnacles, its gates and fountains: all in prayer. Without leaving her village, she had seen the sacred sites people of her day longed to visit. Within a place of prayerful imagination, she had toured the city encircled by mountains, where Jesus himself had walked. Given all that Jerusalem represented, the epitaph probably also meant she found her heart's desire, a deep fulfillment that blessed her final sleep.

Yet many contemporary thinkers share Diarmuid O'Murchu's concern:

> It is at the level of the imagination that contemporary life is weakest. With two-thirds of humanity struggling to meet basic survival needs and the other third largely preoccupied with accumulating and hoarding wealth, the human capacity for reflection, intuition, and the development of the imagination is at an all-time low.[1]

If people are so caught up in jobs and family that life is limited to only what they can sense, that is sadly narrow.

At least two of the people mentioned in chapter 1 as examples were using their imaginations: the artist and the protester. The former imagines a sculpture or a drawing that has never been before; the latter imagines the possibility for a more peaceful future. Without imagination, we could not have hope for something better; psychologists work with people whose imaginations are severely deadened to restore this sense of possibility.

How does the imagination come into play in prayer? Of course the imagination can prompt art, drama, music, and poetry—but *prayer*? Isn't prayer prescribed? How can it be creative?

An answer comes from St. Joan of Arc. She was stunned when the Inquisition rebuked her for believing that God spoke through her imagination. "But how *else* would God speak to me?" she replied in surprise.

One way St. Ignatius of Loyola led people closer to God was by touching their imaginations. He encouraged them to express their "great desires," imagining what astonishing things God might have planned for them.

IMAGINE A BEAUTIFUL COTTAGE

In our day, Robert Wicks imagines prayer as a beautiful cottage on the beach or in the mountains. It's stocked with a full refrigerator, the logs flame in the fireplace, and the deck overlooks a splendid view. Surrounded by acres of pristine forest with endless meandering trails and fields of poppies or columbine, it has easy access to trout streams, ski slopes, golf courses, or tennis courts—pick a favorite activity.

But here's the hitch. We never go there. We never use this second home. We have busy schedules; we get caught up in the demands of work, family, social life. We may long for that cabin nostalgically; we may mentally cast fly rods into its trout streams as we fall asleep at night. But our yearning never changes to action because it's too much trouble. For crying out loud: Who wants to pack up the car and drive an hour?

So the cottage sits, beautiful, inaccessible, gathering dust.

And we spend most of our time in the outer world. Elaborate description is unnecessary; we confront it daily. There we try to earn a living, do some good, make the planet a friendlier place for our children. Yet in that struggle, we often get beaten up. As Jesus predicted, "In the world you will have trouble" (John 16:33). The world chews us up and spits us out, which is why we come home exhausted at night, inordinately grateful for a little food, a little rest.

What's the connection between the outer world and the inner world of prayer? Granted, it's mysterious. But the same Presence who nurtures us in the inner world accompanies us through the outer. The same Someone who is with us in the sunny garden is also with us in the emergency room, the smelly factory, the inept bureaucratic office, and the grocery-store line. If our sense of this Presence is strong enough, it can carry us through the outer places and encounters we detest. It is, after all, the same God—walking both where the jackhammers roar and where the stillness wells. We are, after all, the same people—smelling the meadow full of wildflowers as well as chafing in the meeting that has dragged on an hour too long.

TURNING INWARD

While extraverts may not do this as regularly as introverts do, turning to the inner world can bring relief from delays, bounced checks, failures, hassles, snarling bosses, incompetent clerks, or grumpy children. In that still place, we can meet something—or Someone—who brings immense peace, who sits with us in sunlight where we hear the music of fountains.

If that vision borders on the idealistic or skirts the sentimental, we apply the acid test of prayer: whether it leads to action. What were the Old Testament prophets doing if not imagining another order, where the poor would not be stepped on and the gap between them and the wealthy would not stretch so wide? Didn't Jesus invite people to imagine a world where no one was marginalized, where even the children on the lowest rung of the social ladder were honored? The people of Poland, living beneath the unblinking stare of the communist regime, confronting its military might, might easily have seen an unassailable wall. Instead, they imagined a freer world and, through the work of Solidarity, achieved it. Feminist theologians in our day know the realities of a male-dominated church, exclusive language, and masculine rites. Yet they propose another way, imagine celebrations no one has yet seen, work to implement a vision of equality.

These are only four examples; Anne Kelly summarizes more:

> Within the Christian tradition, sacramental celebrations can be interpreted as the poetic texts that have enabled Christians to imagine newness and possibility, by proposing to the imagination new ways of being in the world. . . . If we are to be a people who can reconstitute the world, we need to be thinking and imagining differently. . . . A love of life and all its processes demands a conversion of the imagination to this new way of seeing. It is a radical reversal of the familiar patterns of domination that are death-dealing to their core. It is a vision of reality as graced to the core. It is an invitation to find that the ordinary is extraordinary.[2]

Walter Brueggemann praises "this outrageous practice of speaking alternative possibility."[3] It stands up to the powers that reduce human life to dullness and conformity, that crank out the same unconvincing slogans. And it announces a better world, new possibilities, "relentless hope."[4]

"See, I am making all things new," says God in the book of Revelation (21:5). Perhaps that process begins with us. An inner transformation means we can see five options where before were only two. Our attitudes can expand; our judgments on other flawed humans can be less harsh; we can learn to soften or strengthen our words. We can imagine ourselves acting in ways that are more sensitive to others' needs, pause to think before we speak, find kinder ways to phrase hard truths, leap more generously to service where we might otherwise hesitate.

The imagination acts like the soul's periscope. "Without an imagination the soul would have no way of communicating with us, no way to pull our attention to its needs, no way to tell us how deeply we are connected to God."[5] It's a reach beyond our usual realm, a way of accessing that which eludes our senses' ways of knowing. It's how we plan the future—we may be caught in a wintry climate, but we can imagine ourselves flying south, boarding a boat, hearing Caribbean waves, feeling the spray in our faces, docking, climbing through masses of bougainvillea to the hotel on rocky crags overlooking the sea. All that mental activity then prompts us to turn what is imagined into what is real—we save the money, call the travel agent, make hotel reservations, and pack.

HOW TO USE THE IMAGINATION IN PRAYER

That's a fairly self-serving example, but it can approximate what happens in prayer. We can reflect prayerfully on any situation, asking ourselves, What are the possibilities here for conversion? for new thinking? for better action? Must I endure the winter for a while (always a possibility), or can I warm the chill? How can I find in this situation the abundant life God wants me to have? We can even ask how our dreams might guide prayer, knowing how they open a window into the soul.

St. Ignatius of Loyola suggests one way to pray with the imagination: by placing ourselves in Scripture stories. He believed that if we could enter the world of Jesus, we could grow closer to him and become more like him. For instance, he asked retreatants to imagine the Trinity looking at the world, seeing all the sadness and horrors that afflict the world's people. While we might expect the Trinity to be angry, they instead are moved with compassion. They decide to send the second person as a human being, and to ask Mary to be Jesus' mother.[6]

We place ourselves imaginatively into the Nativity scene, leaning against a hayrack, perhaps, or petting the donkey. Ignatius envisions many details, culminating in the placing of the tiny baby in our arms. At that point we begin to understand the strength of God's desire to be with human beings. We pray, perhaps welcoming the child, perhaps thanking God, perhaps longing to be closer than we are to Christ. Ignatius invites us to stay with the moment, savoring it, lest we miss any of what it holds for us.

The same strategy could be applied to almost any Gospel story as we take the role of a character, or simply a bystander observing Jesus. Perhaps we are the woman bent double, and look at what forces still keep us from freedom. In prayer we ask ourselves, Where do we need Jesus' healing touch? Perhaps we are the disciples on the road to Emmaus, wondering what good news we can hear from the strangers in our lives, those with whom we normally don't associate. Or we are the good thief, asking a last-minute reprieve from the other crucified criminal.

For those who have never tried this kind of prayer, it may be the ticket to Jerusalem, a chance to walk with Jesus in his earthly setting. No matter what particular kind of imagination we have, God has gifted us all with the ability to join Chione in her imaginative journey.

EFFECTS OF IMAGINATIVE PRAYER

We have already seen how the prayer of imagination spills into action. Remember: "The Christian community has long been a people of memory and imagination. Our remembering and dreaming have long gone hand in hand."[7] We do more than dream, though. Imagining better alternatives, we tutor the illiterate, call leaders to accountability, demand justice, research a cure for AIDS, fund scholarships. What might be some more personal effects of imaginative prayer?

Since several dynamics might occur, let's look at examples of each.

First, in prayer we can reconcile radical opposites. Within most prayers, we can observe dramatic swings of mood, from rage to peace, as people channel their feelings toward God. This passage from Isaiah, for instance, uses exquisite imagery for both ends of the spectrum:

Like a weaver you roll up my life
to cut it from the loom. (38:12)

Eight verses later, the writer has pivoted from finality to eternity:

We will sing to stringed instruments
all the days of our lives,
at the house of the Lord. (38:20)

Either the writer of this passage is fickle or schizophrenic, or he has learned to balance the tension of opposites that characterizes human life. How often in the course of a day do we swing from elation to despair? How can the slightest incident so drastically affect our moods?

Perhaps what the writer of the Isaiah passage has developed, as have many people of prayer, is an attitude, an orientation of the spirit and heart toward God in all things. As the actor Martin Sheen says, "Either I find God in everything, or I find God in nothing." Knowing that everything comes from God's hand, we become convinced not that something will turn out well, but that it will matter, regardless of how it turns out. In the place of prayer we knit together, restore precarious balance, set a direction for the next step.

Second, in prayer we can remember who we are. The Buddhist practice of mindfulness described by Thich Nhat Hanh recalls our joy in being alive and restores our dignity. Through it "I come back to myself," just as the son of the parable realizes how far he's gone astray and "returns to himself." But there's a poverty in the self that pushes us one step further. We need to draw on the marvelous riches of God. We need to discover "prayer as energy, as the energy to enter into deeper relation"[8]—with God, each other, and ourselves.

Third, in prayer we not only restore identity and relationships, we find beauty and buoyancy again. It's ironic that some folks consider religious people dour and grim, dressed always in black, hell-bent on condemning anyone who's having a good time. While that portrait probably fits a dismal few, writers such as Kathleen Norris have corrected the misperception.

The Cloister Walk, her account of life in a monastery, swells with laughter at monastic humor. She gives abundant examples of her perception that "sometimes being a guest in a monastery feels to me like falling comfortably, into a den of playful storytellers."9 From the juxtaposition of ancient and modern come plentiful opportunities for monks to laugh at themselves, a phenomenon she observed frequently over ten years of being a Benedictine oblate. People of faith are quite familiar with the juxtaposition of tragic/comic, sublime/banal, ideal/real that constitutes human life and forms the basis for humor.

Using the imagination in prayer, then, can open broader windows on our own lives. It can help us draw closer to God, recognize God's hand at play, restore our true identity and right relationship to others.

Compare this sojourn in prayer to the time spent in the scenic cabin. Aren't we more relaxed, more appreciative, easier to be with, more centered on what matters after a vacation? Could prayer that exercises the imagination have some similar effects?

REFLECT

What is your initial response to the use of the imagination in prayer as described in this chapter? ◆ *Recall a time when you imagined a better solution and achieved it.*

PRAY

Creator God, you gave me the gift of imagination. Now guide me in its use.

16

TAMING THE WOLF

A Channel to Peace

*Peace comes from not needing to control everything
and not needing to have everything and
not needing to surpass everyone and not needing to
know everything and not needing to have
everyone else be like me. Peace comes from seeking God
in the present and seeing the world as a whole.*

—JOAN CHITTISTER

Franciscan author Richard Rohr has portrayed the contemporary person as weighted down with pain and anxiety. "Help me deal with constant crisis!" seems to be our slogan. But Rohr raises the stakes higher, challenging: If our spirituality doesn't offer a way to transform our pain, we'll pass the suffering on to others. Humans have a huge capacity to project blame, because it's so much easier than doing the inner work of transformation. Thus, our inner life can assume a global dimension; from the unresolved pain of one person can issue the wars that devastate nations.

The Christian looks toward Jesus for a way out of this tangle. He told people that the opposite of faith wasn't doubt; it was fear, anxiety, worry about many things. Christ came to free us from that muddle. Faith in him gives us the ability to hold a certain degree of tension without expelling it on someone else. If we don't give it over to God, we'll transmit it.

LIVING IN A DRIVEN SOCIETY

Rohr explains why so many North Americans have a messiah complex: if we can't believe God's in charge, we'd be irresponsible *not* to take charge, to try to fix and control everything—or at least to get compulsive about the little we can control, making sure the wastebaskets are empty and the pencils sharpened!

His theory makes considerable sense. But where do we take it? If we are going to let go, if we are going to give up our constant preoccupation with tinkering, fixing, manipulating, we'll need some help. This tendency is, after all, deeply rooted in the take-charge people who built the transcontinental railroad, invented cars and penicillin, created computers and fiber optics and space travel. The urge to get it right is enshrined by the culture, praised by good parents, and rewarded in high achievers.

For us to let God be in charge thus takes some doing. Anything that smacks of surrender is not an easy maneuver for Western people. Releasing, trusting, letting go don't come naturally. We are contentious; we challenge; we fret. Only infrequently do our universities give honorary doctorates to contemplatives. Programmed into almost every North American child is the imperative: hurry up, compete, win, make Mom and Dad proud. Rarely do we encourage our children to simply be. We invite them to join us on the treadmill to success, preferably at the same pace we're trudging.

Clearly, we'll need some help if we are going to relax our ambitions. If we intend to bite our tongues during committee meetings when the words of criticism rise easily to the lips, if we want to address our colleagues and families in nonthreatening, nonjudgmental ways, then we need a resolve that is beyond human limits.

Lord knows, our trials are enough to sink the saints. On a daily basis, we go through minor martyrdoms and tiny tortures. Not to respond in kind is superhuman. Precisely. It requires a transformation, the kind that can be wrought only by the slow, quiet alchemy of prayer.

TRANSFORMING FEAR AND FRENZY

It's not impossible—remember the story of St. Francis and the wolf of Gubbio. Fear and frenzy permeated the village, because the wolf was devouring the livestock. The townspeople feared that they or their children would be next on the menu. But the wolf was simply hungry, a natural enough state for a wolf. Francis spoke to him softly, gave him something to eat, and directed a dazzled audience to continue feeding the wolf regularly.

In so doing, Francis showed all of us how to handle the wolves that howl without and devour within. Anyone watching Francis's behavior would suspect he spent considerable time in the presence of God before he entered the frantic community of humans. Not that the Gubbians didn't have a legitimate need. Anyone who would deny the existence of genuine wolves in our world is either naive or insulated from reality.

But Francis did what Thich Nhat Hanh recommends: treat anger and fear as a mother would hold a screaming child. Ignoring the cries does not quiet them, but quiet attention calms them.[1] "It is best not to say, 'Go away, Fear. I don't like you. You are not me.' It is much more effective to say, 'Hello, Fear. How are you today?'"[2] When we are at peace with ourselves, our negative emotions no longer run rampant or dominate. We identify them almost casually—Ah, fear. There you are again.

Francis also did what Richard Rohr suggests: turn the problem over to God. Knowing that this one was beyond human limits, he invited God's help—and got it. The fact that we are surprised when God helps us says volumes about our lack of trust, our cynicism, our unwillingness to be helped, even by the divine. Francis was caught up in the superhuman, as we all can be. He participated in graces that are accessible to any of us, God being an equal-opportunity gracer.

If we enter our homes or workplaces with our needs seething and our untouched longings screaming, we can easily burden our families and friends with our agendas. While narcissism may be legitimate at two, it's less acceptable at twenty, and downright unfashionable at fifty. Anyone who's worked with an adolescent forty-year-old knows how wearing it gets—yet sometimes we're patient because we recognize our unredeemed self squirming there. Don't we all have legitimate grounds for anxiety, undeniable stresses, burdens we don't know how to cope with?

Where else can we take all that angst, if not to prayer? Sure, a sympathetic friend helps, a spouse might bear some of the mutual burden, laughter soothes, and family supports, but still we wonder where to lay this weight.

CHRIST: HERO AND COMPANION

The answer looks out at us from the cross. Jesus took that suffering, "once and for all," according to Paul, and transformed it. He never said a word about hurt in his postresurrection appearances. He simply encouraged his followers not to be afraid. He had faced the worst they would ever encounter, stared it down, and defeated it for them.

Perhaps that's why other eras referred to Christ as the champion, the chevalier. It's not a modern image; we skitter from the suggestion of triumphalism. But there it is, undeniable: he beat our worst enemies. He is, in the fullest sense of the word, a hero. We stand before the instrument of his torture humbled, and at the same time honored. When we hang on our personal crosses, feeling the weight in our sagging arms, we aren't alone.

Rohr has pointed out that Jesus was crucified on the collision of opposites. He paid the price inside himself for their coming together. Jesus' two nailed hands show what it takes to hold the two sides of every question—male/female, gay/straight, liberal/conservative, all our polarities. He creates a "world in between"—the kingdom of God, where no one stands on certitude or superiority. The cross tells us that the ultimate pattern of reality is cruciform, filled with contradiction.

It shouldn't take long to discover that pattern in our daily experience. Many people deal with ideals/realities, money/intangibles, enemies/friends, and a host of other contradictions before noon. If that's not enough to start the inner turmoil, the day plays out with continued contradiction: I really want to be doing this; instead, I am doing that. I have ten minutes for this conversation; instead, I give it an hour. My finest self would do one thing; my animal instincts do another. My heart is at home; my body is at the factory. My child deserves my time; I spend it on work.

No wonder I'm ready to scream at the first person who sneezes! It's probably miraculous there isn't more homicide, road rage, and general hysteria. How do we contain the tensions? How might the polarities of an ordinary day be reconciled in prayer?

RECONCILING THE DAY'S TENSIONS

Let's assume that prayer opens and punctuates the day. While that may sound unrealistic if we think of prayer only in traditional terms, it is what we mean by the attitude of prayer. Rather than another duty to add to an overly long list, prayer permeates the atmosphere like a gentle rain, misting the sharp corners, softening the hard clods of earth, greening the surfaces.

Let's say, further, that today's prayer was a meditation on peace, a quiet considering of how to disarm the heart. The one who prays invites God's presence into situations where a sharp sword seems the only recourse. The ideal is immediately challenged when the first item on the agenda is a meeting with a co-worker whose laugh has a hyenalike ring, whose abilities are below par, whose arrogance is unremitting. (If prayer means anything, shouldn't it be tested in a worst-case scenario?)

One-Who-Prays takes a deep breath and asks God for the wisdom to know when to challenge, when to let go, when to voice concern, when to affirm. Recognizing the futility of argument, the pray-er knows that getting upset will only cost her: her backache, her migraine, her time; the co-worker will sail into the next meeting unscathed. The pray-er slips into the memory of the morning, those few moments with sunlight on the face and stillness all around. At that time, she knew herself beloved by God; that's really all that matters.

She also reminds herself that Karl Rahner, Jesuit priest and theologian, defined every human being as "God's absolute, radical self-revelation." Seeking that revelation definitely enlivens a dull meeting, turns it into a scavenger hunt for glimmers of divinity in co-workers.

At this point the efficiency experts get concerned: With all this rumination, how much attention is being paid to the work at hand? Remember that the goal here is not to cheat the employer, but to bring peace into the marketplace. In the long run, a peaceful working environment benefits the employer. And does anything achieve it as well as employees who are at peace with themselves? Does anything bring them to that place as effectively as prayer at the day's beginning, prayer remembered periodically, prayer invoked throughout the day?

One reason for the popularity of Celtic prayer is its steady regularity. Each happening in the day, from milking the cow to

making the beer to stirring the fire, had its own special blessing. Invoking God's presence so often invites "the peace of
Christ above all peace." So does the certainty of walking everywhere with the Trinity:

Father above me;
Son beside me;
Spirit within me;
The Three all around me. [3]

Those who as children prayed to Matthew, Mark, Luke, and
John like four sturdy posters of a bed may find the same solidi-
ty in the fourfold invocation to God: "Hear, hold, love, enfold."
Like a mantra, the repeated words can spiral around us.

The notion of prayer as comfort has some unsettling conno-
tations of meat loaf, rice pudding, and other foods we're supposed to eat when we're hurting. Yet many of us turn to prayer
regularly because we have found there great consolation. If we
return again and again and are satisfied, who's to criticize?
Perhaps prayer as a channel to peace is only a slightly more
sophisticated version of the same concept.

As always, we can look to the model of Jesus. Aware of how
little time he has before his passion, he washes the feet of his
disciples. It is the soothing, cleansing action of a peacemaker,
especially since the treacherous Judas is still present at supper.
John comments on Jesus' quiet certitude: he knew "that he had
come from God and was returning to God" (John 13:3).

What else does anyone need to know? That conviction carried Jesus through a brutal ordeal, and that conviction can be

ours. We too have come from God and will return to God. What more do we need for inner peace?

REFLECT

St. Francis's Prayer for Peace is famous. What might be the connections between it and his encounter with the wolf of Gubbio? ◆ *What "wolves" gnaw at you, within or without? How do you treat them?*

PRAY

God who can bring peace to war-torn countries, create your peace within me. From that still center, may I spread peace to others.

17

PRAYER IN PARALYSIS

The Voice of Grief

Alas, dear Christ, the Dragon is here again.

—St. Gregory Nazianzus

For Gregory, the monster was too overwhelming for any sword to slay. For us, the phrases marking hopeless finality have the ring of a gate clanging shut. End of the rope. Closed door. Dead end. Last gasp. Final stop. We slam hard against our human limitations, and that's that. No more energy, solutions, time, or innovation to channel there. "There" might mean a relationship, a job, a church, any arena that once nurtured and now is sadly devoid of life.

It may take a process of repeated bumping against the harsh reality for the news to penetrate: this corpse is cold. This trail has vanished. This fuse has fizzled; this surge is spent; this account is bankrupt. What's next? Sometimes, if we're wise, we pray. Chapter 1 includes a cameo of a husband beside his wife's hospital bed. Prayer was his response to her diagnosis.

AT THE END OF THE ROPE

It may be a sad comment on our relationship to the divine, but we often go to prayer when we have nowhere else to turn. Our sense of loss is overwhelming; our future direction is deadened. Perhaps prayer is the only way to fully explore the loss; any other approach, like pressure on a stinging burn, would be unbearable.

Psalm 88 articulates the stark loneliness of one who stands so abjectly before God:

I am reckoned as one in the tomb:
I have reached the end of my strength, . . .

like those you remember no more,
cut off . . . from your hand. (5)

I have borne your trials; I am numb. (15)

Friend and neighbor you have taken away:
my one companion is darkness. (18)

A friend, spiritual director, or counselor may be helpful in a crisis and may even lead us to the verge of prayer. Then, when all other human channels fail, prayer takes over, the authentic voice of our grief. Only in prayer can we prod the exact nature of the loss and come to bear it. Only in prayer can we go around, or through, or over, the confines of our human selves.

Many self-help books assure us that we may not be able to change the hand we've been dealt, but we can choose how to live with it. The experts remind us that smelly, rotting garbage fertilizes fragrant flowers. It's stalwart advice, but the Christian wants more. The Christian recognizes truth here, but wants a more personal dimension, wants this insight placed in the context of the Christ story, wants that conversation around the compost heap to turn to prayer.

PARALYSIS TOUCHED BY CHRIST

One approach might be to place ourselves in the story told in Mark 2:1–12 of the paralyzed man brought to Jesus on a stretcher by four friends. Unable to reach him because of the crowd clustered at the door, they dig through the roof, create an opening, and lower the paralytic down to Jesus. It's worth pausing to imagine the grin of surprise and delight on Jesus' face as he watched this strange carriage descending.

It's also important to note the role that others can play when we are incapable of movement. The four friends take the initiative; confronting obstacles, they become creative and succeed with a burst of ingenuity quite beyond the reach of their paralyzed friend. It's interesting to note that the story begins when Jesus is "at home" and concludes when he tells the healed person to "stand up, take your mat and go to your home" (11). Many of us might ask in bewilderment, "Where's home?" Others may help us find the answer. In the Christian community, no one must go it alone.

Convinced that we have an advocate who knows our distress firsthand, we ask with the psalmist to "let the bones that you have crushed rejoice" (51:8). The Christian clings to the consolation that one whose own bones were so recklessly broken must hear such a plea with sympathy. In a state of paralysis, the Christian knows only one place to go, one way to turn, one face and voice to seek: that of the suffering Christ. Our identification with Christ begins to offer a way out, a walk through, a meaning that relieves brute suffering. In prayer we try to take on his mind, his spirit. Because he has survived the dire extremes, he can accompany us there. In the quiet of meditation, we draw on his strength.

IDENTIFYING WITH CHRIST

To better understand how this might happen, let's look at two depictions of this prayerful identification, one in fiction, one in Scripture. In Wallace Stegner's novel *Crossing to Safety*, the narrator's wife, Sally, is paralyzed from polio and moves painfully on crutches. He describes an outing in Italy when the couple and their friends see a painting of the resurrected Christ that reveals lingering, shocking details of his crucifixion.

> *Until then there had been a good deal of frivolity in us, a springtime response to the blossoms and the mild, clear air. But Piero's Christ knocked it out of us like an elbow in the solar plexus. That gloomy, stricken face permitted no forgetful high spirits. It was not the face of a god reclaiming his suspended immortality, but the face of a man who until a moment ago had been thoroughly and horribly dead, and still had the smell of death in his clothes and the terror of death in his mind. If resurrection had taken place, it had not yet been comprehended. . . . And what terrible eyes this Christ had!*[1]

One friend, who is developing a "sundial theory of art, which would count no hours but the sunny ones," criticizes the picture roundly. But the narrator notices his wife standing on her crutches before it for a long time. He comments, "She studied it soberly, with something like recognition or acknowledgment in her eyes, as if those who have been dead understand things that will never be understood by those who have only lived."[2] Sally has been in the same place as Christ, has been buried with him, and can understand him far better than those who float happily and smoothly on the surface.

An example from Luke 24:13–35 models another way this process of identification with Christ can happen. The story begins in the "stuck" stance that's all too familiar. Two disciples on the road to Emmaus hit the wall described above: "They stopped short," says Luke's Gospel. They are paralyzed by sorrow: their hopes in Jesus and their brief, dim glimpse of self-transformation have been nailed to a cross, left to die miserably. Joined by a stranger on the road, they are dumbfounded when he asks what they are discussing. Is he the village idiot, who doesn't have a clue about the local ferment?

Jesus is apparently not averse to mucking around in the compost and, in this case, playing dumb. When he encourages the pair to talk, they start moving again (the first perk of Presence). About their ensuing conversation, Henri Nouwen says, "The stranger didn't say that there was no reason for sadness, but that their sadness was part of a larger sadness in which joy was hidden."[3] While the disciples refer to rumors that the women in their group found the tomb empty, they do not give them much credence. It is only when they eat with the risen Lord that they recognize him, and at that moment he disappears.

Nouwen underscores the significance of his timing: the physical absence leads to a spiritual presence. Because the disciples have eaten the bread of Jesus' life, they are transformed into him. Our communion with each other and with Christ "is so intimate, so holy, so sacred and so spiritual that our corporeal senses can no longer reach it. . . . He has come to us at that place within us where the powers of darkness and evil cannot reach, where death has no access."[4]

Jesus is no stranger to this place of darkness. That he knew the place well is evident in his cry from the cross, "My God, my God, why hast thou forsaken me?" As Martin Marty writes, the cry assures us that in our darkest times we are not alone. "Someone in whom I trust has shouted it out before, in worse circumstances. . . . The rest of us die in company, in *his* company. . . . Never again is aloneness to be so stark for others."[5]

In other words, the redemptive suffering of Christ dispels the death-dealing forces that create our various forms of paralysis. Through prayer, we tap into a force beyond anything human, entering into lives that are clearly constrained by human limitations. Once again, the stone rolls away from the entrance to the tomb, perhaps one gradual chunk at a time. Then the power of his resurrection triumphs again, this time in us.

A RESURRECTED POWER

Because this complete transformation could easily be misinterpreted as "pie in the sky," let's approach it through various lenses. The poet Robin Behn could be addressing Jesus when writing:

> But all you ever wanted
> was to vanish into our midst.[6]

Behn alludes to the fact that Jesus' resurrection allows him to be everywhere, even with us in our darkest swamp. We may long to touch and see and hear him, but deprived of the usual sensate channels, we can experience him in other ways: through prayer, for instance. His healing may seep into our broken limbs when we thought we were only wasting time in an empty silence.

Writers exploring quantum theory and its relevance to theology tell us that creation is part of a larger whole, greater than the sum of the parts.[7] Just as the structure of each atomic particle parallels the design of the constellations, so all humanity makes up the body of Christ. Yes, we are unique individuals, but yes—and alleluia!—our identity is also part of a greater one where we are united with each other and Christ.

In the context of the Emmaus story, the pain was brutally true, unmistakable as welts or nail marks. But it was also part of a longer narrative, introduced by the women's testimony about resurrection. So we who see only a fraction cannot guess in what larger arenas we act. We cannot imagine how the vibrations from one stone in the water affect waves on distant shores. To pray is to enter the deep silence that hints at a broader scope.

The language of ordinary people reveals that it is only when we have the strong grip of God's hands around ours that we can muster the courage to grasp reality. When our little lives are held fast in the embrace of a greater God, we can begin to face squarely the pain that we have caused others and that others have caused us. God's presence around us is like a second skin, strengthening and protecting, or a film of oil screening us from an overdose of sun.

THE TESTIMONY OF SURVIVORS

The most convincing testimony always comes from people who have been there. It's not unusual to hear a person who has endured a crisis say, "Without God, I could never have gotten through the ordeal. But I put my hand in God's each day, through each step, and I survived." Prayer, then, seems to lead not to a solution, but to a presence and peace, a conviction that we're not in this alone.

In prayer, we may find ourselves danced in a larger pattern or placed in a longer story. Where we've been landed may be beyond our control. But learning the pattern in which we're danced, the music in which we're sung, comes from long periods of silence and contemplation. To be caught up in the passive voice does not come easily to most North Americans. It takes time getting used to this larger whole, this belonging to a body that is not physical.

If we can make that leap, we no longer feel paralyzed, but become like the woman Elizabeth Jennings describes: "She was the peace her prayer had promised."[8] Within us, then, when we are joined to Christ, can be the sword Gregory needed, the handle to open locked doors, the jolt of energy to dead bones.

REFLECT

When have you experienced a paralysis similar to that described in this chapter? How were you freed, or do you still endure it? ◆ *Do you find the rationale of this chapter convincing? Why or why not?*

PRAY

With the poet May Sarton, we pray: "Give me, O God, to be in your presence, even when I feel it only as absence."

18

THE SAINTS

A Conversation

among Friends

From silly devotions and sour-faced saints,
good Lord deliver us!
—St. Teresa of Avila

After a hellish workday in which company management again demonstrated their short-sightedness, a co-author dropped out of a key project, the mail contained harsh criticism, and the computer shut down every time I pressed the print key, I picked up a child and rushed through the grocery store. We got home breathless at 5 P.M., but we weren't done yet. Dinner guests were due at six; some fast and furious cooking, cleaning, and table setting lay ahead. The situation called for superhuman intervention. I closed the door of my room for five minutes and imagined a conversation with three friends who had died in the last year. All had been working moms; all would relate to my plight. In an unofficial variation on the litany of the saints, I pleaded with Judy, Elizabeth, and Jill. "Give me some quick energy. Let the dinner party go well."

At the risk of sounding superstitious, I must say that the evening went better than a few where I've spent most of the day preparing. Guests were relaxed, chatted amiably, and even asked for seconds on the pasta. The chef basked in compliments, knowing how closely she'd skirted disaster. Reflecting that night on the day's highlights, I had to admit that those five minutes behind the closed door were pivotal. Perhaps it is natural to evoke the spirits of those we have loved in this life; one friend swears that her long-deceased mother expertly finds her a parking place in the worst downtown traffic.

THE COMMUNITY OF SAINTS

Before this disintegrates into a misperception of prayer as bargaining, let's look at a broader notion of union with the dead called the communion of saints. In this company are joined the living and dead, the officially canonized and those whose sanctity is enshrined only in a few remembering hearts. Membership in this club is open to all and creates for the living a broad circle of support, freeing us at some level from the restrictions of being one human at one time in one place.

G. K. Chesterton describes the attraction: "I belong to the Catholic church, a deep and rich tradition, to avoid the terrible servitude of being a child of my time." Commenting on Chesterton, Father Michael Himes of Boston College rejoices that this communion can't even be interrupted by a minor detail such as death. "As with voting in Cook County," he quipped in a lecture, "death doesn't disqualify."

Geddes MacGregor in *The Rhythm of God* tells of a priest who, when asked, "How many people were at the early celebration of the Eucharist last Wednesday morning?" replied, "There were three old ladies, the janitor, several thousand archangels, a large number of seraphim, and several million of the triumphant saints of God."[1] Such a "cloud of witnesses" answers a deep human urge to be part of something larger, to not stand alone, to give our little lives meaning. One drop of water, left alone, evaporates quickly. But one drop of water in the immense sea endures.

While many people cherish the memories of deceased family members or friends, it's a greater leap to enter the larger circle of people we didn't know when they were alive. But learning about these holy ones is an invaluable help to anyone trying to live fully and reflectively. Like a little girl watching Jackie Joyner-Kersee win awards for running, we can say, "She did it, and she is human like me! Maybe I can do it too!" Our high calling is, after all, to be a saint, and as Leon Bloy says, "There is only one sorrow—not to be a saint."[2]

Most people are quick to define what they want to achieve in a career. "I'll be an architect or an engineer, a sculptor or a CEO," we declare with conviction early in life. Yet with regard to our ultimate destiny, the purpose for which we were made, we are more hesitant. We can easily identify with the young Thomas Merton, asked by his friend Bob Lax, "What do you want to be, anyway?" His initial reply was lame: "A good Catholic." Lax quickly corrected him: "What you should say is that you want to be a saint."

Merton recalls: "'A saint!' The thought struck me as a little weird. I said, 'How do you expect me to become a saint?' 'By wanting to,' said Lax, simply."

The young Merton, prone to drama and insecurity, is astonished that anything could be so easy. Yet as he reflects, Lax's words ring true: "Don't you believe that God will make you what he created you to be, if you will consent to let him do it? All you have to do is desire it."[3]

How logical. We can become what we were born for, by cooperating with the creator's intention. Yet the concept of sainthood seems to have grown barnacles; it's become far more complex than a simple desire. Why? One problem with some accounts of the saints is that they overwhelm us by their miseries and martyrdoms, their single-mindedness that borders on neurosis. We can easily fall into the trap of comparing their trials with ours, a process that inevitably makes us look like saps.

If the hagiography serves only to depress us, it's missed its mark. The heroic stories are meant to show that the saints didn't have smooth sailing through this life either. In their trials and humanness, they are much like us. And if they cooperated with God, so can we. We too can rise above the poverty of the self to be larger, stronger, more generous, *better* than we usually are. As Merton said years later:

> *I have become convinced that the very contradictions in my life are in some way signs of God's mercy to me: if only because someone so complicated and so prone to confusion and self-defeat could hardly survive for long without special mercy.* [4]

In this chapter, we'll explore two ways that the desire to be a saint might become more concrete, enfleshed: by borrowing the saints' words, and by invoking their spirits in prayer.

LEARNING THE LINGO

The infinite variety found in nature echoes in the variety of saints: by myriad paths, different personality types from different places and times have found God. We can thus draw from a rich treasury of saints' words to match the whole varied collage of our own experiences. While it's not quite as simplistic as the charts found in older editions of the Bible ("in despair, read passage X; in doubt, read passage Y"), human needs seem fairly perennial. Only a few examples are tapped here; hundreds more remain unexplored. Let's begin with a prayer for the journey, courteous words of St. Clare of Assisi that are directed toward one's own soul:

> *Go forth in peace, for you have followed the good road. Go forth without fear, for [God] who created you has made you holy, has always protected you, and loves you as a mother.*

One who borrows Clare's words must desire some of her positive spirit: the trust in a good God and a good universe, the confidence that even bad mistakes haven't bumped us off "the good road," the joy of the journey, the motherly welcome of the homecoming. Clare's prayer was so much a part of her, it echoed in her dying words. The sisters at her deathbed were puzzled when they heard her whispering, "Go calmly in peace, for you will have a good escort." When they asked to whom she was speaking, she answered, "To my soul."[5]

Even from the distance of another continent and century, we wish we could know the woman who spoke so nobly and serenely, who became "a clear stream of God's bounty."[6] Similarly, reading her friend St. Francis's Prayer for Peace or Canticle of the Sun, we try to absorb some of his wonder at creation and compassion for all creatures. When we are thrust into situations where we don't want to be, we turn to Francis's *Last Testament* and his pivotal time among the lepers:

> *It seemed too bitter a thing even to look at lepers, and the Lord himself led me among them, and I worked mercy together with them. And when I left them, that which had before seemed bitter was now changed for me into sweetness of soul and body.*[7]

Whenever it rains, I recall Thomas Merton's poem-prayer:

> *What a thing it is to sit absolutely alone, in the forest at night, cherished by this wonderful, unintelligible, perfectly innocent speech, the most comforting speech in the world, the talk that rain makes by itself all over the ridges. As long as it talks, I am going to listen.*[8]

Before a day that I know will be filled with personal interactions, not the strong suit of an introvert like me, I use Catherine de Hueck Doherty's words to open my eyes to the deeper meaning the multiple encounters entail:

Perfect prayer seeks the presence of Christ and recognizes it in every human face. The unique image of Christ is the ikon, but every human face is an ikon of Christ, discovered by a prayerful person.[9]

When I'm tempted to shortchange the voice on the phone that is consuming too much time, to dismiss interruptions brusquely, to avoid the loquacious co-worker, to refuse family members and turn to pressing projects, to take refuge in books that don't talk back, the words sometimes come like an echo. Might I find in this person the icon of Christ? How might I feed this person's hunger?

Perhaps using the saints' words is the first step toward participating in their company. Like a Berlitz course crammed before a trip abroad, prayer is the language of the realm, its coin or currency. It places on our lips ideas we would struggle to articulate, thoughts we might never otherwise have. Just as a lover might borrow the words of a poet to impress the beloved, so we use the prayers of the saints to elevate our discourse with God. Not that we need to impress God, who has heard it all before. But sometimes we become what we admire.

Hearing the saints' words echoing down the ages is another way to appreciate their humanity. They are less off-putting when we realize they could snarl, procrastinate, joke, and fume just as we do. Many have empathized with St. Augustine's plea to God, "Make me chaste—but not yet."

Others have warmed to the wit of St. Thomas More, who ascended the scaffold joking to his executioner, "Assist me up, if you please. Coming down I can shift for myself." He further asked the man to spare his beard, which had caused the king no harm. With admirable farsightedness, he addressed the lords who had condemned him to death: "So I verily trust, and shall therefore right heartily pray, that though your lordships have now here on earth been judges of my condemnation, we may yet hereafter in heaven merrily meet together."[10]

Who, feeling fragile, would not be cheered by St. Teresa of Avila's stalwart encouragement, "Let's not imagine that we are hollow inside"?[11] We who cave in too easily, spoiling those we love, identify with her admission, "I'm defenseless against affection. I could be bribed by a sardine."

We parents nod in empathy with St. Elizabeth Ann Seton, agonizing over her irresponsible teenage sons, and read with delight that in her later years, she drank plenty of port wine.

We who fail often are awed by the admission of Martin Niemoeller, whose heroic resistance to the Nazis cost him years in concentration camps. Yet he regretted that he had not spoken out earlier, louder, for the rights of the Jews. He saw in retrospect that through their suffering, Christ had been asking him, "Are you prepared to save me?" Sadly, Niemoeller admitted, "I turned that service down."[12]

For us, the plea may no longer come through oppressed Jews; it may weave through the voices of family members, patients, students or clients, the homeless or abused, those orphaned by war, brutalized by government, or cheated by corporations. With the same sadness, we might also admit to turning down the service of Christ. In the saints we find patterns of similarity as well as striking uniqueness. While all were driven by the same desire, they responded to specific challenges with their own originality.

CALLING ON THEIR COMPANY

"The saints preserve us!" was the constant cry of the Irish grandmother, and to many the thought of turning to deceased heroes may seem quaint and archaic. We classify this practice with vigil lights and novenas, customs that once nurtured but have been discarded along with manual typewriters and white gloves.

Yet how many celebrities do we enshrine in wax museums, how many baseball pitchers and rodeo winners are honored in halls of fame? Some underlying instinct persists: we want to place ourselves, even if it's only imaginatively, in the company of those who succeeded. Transferring that instinct to the spiritual life, it makes sense to ask the help of those who've dealt with burdens like ours and survived. We want to hang around with kindred sorts who lift our spirits and teach us something of God in human limbs. Perhaps it's the equivalent of placing our hands and feet in the prints left by Hollywood stars in front of Grauman's Chinese Theater. We don't necessarily fit; we just want to try shadowing.

This theory has of course been carried to bizarre extremes, with lists of saints established for various causes, including the patron saint of hemorrhoids. After we've all had a good yuk over the abuses, can we then salvage something useful from the practice?

Without consulting a chart, for instance, I know where to turn when I'm exhausted. With some measure of glee, I think of Catherine of Siena evading a couple who pleaded with her to heal their daughter, who was plagued by evil spirits. She crawled on the roof to escape, asking, "Don't I have enough troubles of my own?"

When I'm up against male arrogance, I like to remember Catherine puncturing that bubble with gusto, in rich, learned, powerful men, including the pope. Her friend and mentor Raymond of Capua would doze off during her talks. As she shook him awake, she'd ask loudly, "Do you really want to miss things useful to your soul, just for the sake of sleep? Am I supposed to be talking to you or the wall?"[13]

When I long for peace and quiet, I remember Catherine's story of crossing the threshold of her private room, leaving her solitude to join her twenty-four siblings and their extended families—noisy, Italian, passionate, and argumentative. She imagined Christ saying, "Go, it is dinner time. Go and join them."[14]

Carol Lee Flinders's book *At the Root of This Longing* begins with a beautiful description of a woman invoking the saints. The woman was "desperately unhappy," so she appealed in daily meditation to a few favorites: "Be here for me now—yes, you—and stay the night, and walk me through my days." She had studied their lives and knew that they had endured their own dark nights. A Christian "only in the broadest sense of the word, . . . she knew without question that the very extremity of her plight—her terrible thirst—was sufficient claim." So, the author concludes, have women always drawn their saints "into the circle of their need."[15]

What may seem magical or superstitious is rooted in honest hunger—or Merton's desire. We cannot discount a practice so full of yearning, a desire to be more, no matter how bizarre it may seem in some of its manifestations. We pay attention when a celebrity endorses a product; if we buy those tennis shoes or wear that line of clothing, we can be as fast as the athlete or as svelte as the movie star who touts their benefits. How then can we not tap into the tremendous body of stories, the enormous wealth and strength left like a legacy by the saints?

REFLECT

Of all the saints mentioned in this chapter, or among your personal favorites, to which one are you most drawn? ◆ How do you pray in the words of this saint? ◆ How do you invoke this saint's help when you are in a situation similar to one the saint experienced?

PRAY

Choose the words or the model of a favorite saint, canonized or un-. Invoke this person as the day begins and unfolds. Return to this holy company at night and ask, How has this companionship made a difference today?

19

IN CLOSING

A Calendar

.

To see Thee is the End and the Beginning
Thou carriest me and thou goest before.
Thou are the journey and the journey's end.
—ATTRIBUTED TO KING ALFRED

One wonders: Did King Alfred have a Day-Timer? Probably not, but most of us do. Sometimes we're more tied to it than we'd care to admit. On the positive side, we can seek in calendar pages avenues to prayer. We can find the concrete working-out of Alfred's suggestion that God is there all along, in beginnings and ends, in prepositions like "during" and "afterward," in "here" and "not yet," in arduous journeys and glad arrivals.

It may not be the first prayer prompt that springs to mind, this calendar or book that dictates our days, directs our waking hours, and causes havoc if it's ever lost. We may regard it more as a necessary evil, telling us when we have meetings, doctor appointments, haircuts, and, every now and then, a rare blank space in which to breathe. Some might harrumph that overloaded calendars are symptomatic of everything that's wrong with a frenzied lifestyle: driven days and packed moments, too much jammed into the small squares of a week, crises so scheduled that nothing spontaneous could ever erupt.

Perhaps the critics are right. Where could we ever squeeze God in, when we must plot with our friends for three months in advance to arrange an hour together? Some people even schedule "quality time" with their children. How, then, is there ever room for contemplation, for cloud staring, for the impromptu? Where are the empty deserts in which seekers have traditionally found the space and leisure to contemplate and meditate?

CONTEMPLATING THE CALENDAR

Such questions are valid, but they cannot be considered in the abstract. Perhaps the best answers, the only real answers come from taking the time to page through a calendar and reflect on its contents. It's not a daily exercise, but one better suited to a birthday, an anniversary, or New Year's Eve. The pages on which we meditate may seem checkered, but they are the stuff and substance of our lives. Prayer over a calendar might explicitly reveal the traces of God's presence in our days.

For people who place a high value on their time, the calendar describes the treasure on which they have set their hearts. It's convenient to have a written record of our highest values and to see God's actions interwoven with ours. The divine designs in the calendar may not be immediately apparent, but they reveal themselves over time. "For surely I know the plans I have for you, says the LORD, plans for your welfare and not for harm, to give you a future with hope" (Jeremiah 29:11).

Now wait a minute, our friendly local skeptic may interject. Surely an appointment with the dentist or car mechanic doesn't represent the be-all and end-all of my days? Surely there's more to *me* than my functions? That's exactly what the calendar may reveal.

THE CALENDAR'S PATHS TO PRAYER

As we glance through its squares, we find many paths to prayer we recognize. Work and work-related commitments consume a huge percentage of the calendar. But we know that work can be a channel through which God co-creates, makes us more human, develops our gifts, and enables us to serve others. We may not see immediate results, but they hover between the lines, float mysteriously through the pages of the calendar. If we actually saw all the fruits of our labors, we might be impossible to live with, full of self-congratulation and overblown ego. On the other hand, if we actually saw all our failures, projects misdirected or aborted, time misspent, hours wasted, we might be too sunk in depression to continue.

So we look through this record with the lens of faith, knowing that our professional, social, and religious lives are all interrelated. As Vatican II reminded us, "Religion and everyday life are intimately and indissolubly linked, part and parcel of each other. We cannot divorce what happens in religion from how we live our everyday life. Simply put, there is no split between faith and everyday life."[1]

As we continue paging through the calendar, we may come upon some entries that bewilder. What does "lunch with M" mean? Why did we block out a whole weekend for "T's play"? Why does a long weekend have nothing but a reservation number written on it?

With a little thought, it may come back. Remember? "M" had recently lost her job. She was at loose ends with too much time to fill. It was a frantic week, but we met for a salad. She verbally flogged her former boss and sketched out her plans for a job search. And who knows how much good it did her, to be listened into healing, to be befriended into the next small step toward the future.

Then that puzzling annotation about "T's play . . . " Ah yes. The shy daughter or nephew who for the first time performed in the school play. She or he spent 587 hours practicing one line. For some obscure reason, we went to all three performances. Will it go into some cosmic calculator, tipping the balance of good and evil in the world? Probably not. Did it reassure a child that someone cared enough to come? Did the applause ring like music in that child's ears? We'll probably never know; let's chalk it up to "sowing seed."

Not that we, like raving codependents, are always on the giving end. Sprinkled on the calendar are instances where we were the receivers of time others could ill afford. What about the doctor appointment at 5:30 P.M. on Christmas Eve, when the pediatrician gave a welcome dose of penicillin so a son didn't have to endure Christmas with strep throat? Or the counselor who squeezed us in even though it meant working overtime . . . or the friend who wasted time with us just because we needed to talk . . . or the job interview that we were desperate to get . . . or the visit of a dear relative we had not seen in years . . . or the teacher conference that cleared up many questions about a child's poor performance in school . . . or the watercolor class on Tuesday evening that became an island of sanity . . . or the monthly meeting with a spiritual director or support group . . . The list continues as our calendar review fills us with a deep and heartfelt gratitude. Indeed, there are saints among us who minister to our most awkward, pressing, ill-expressed needs. What a gift to have them!

Some expenditures of time benefit both of those who share it. That explains the space labeled "Reservation #6942R." A friend had just gotten divorced, and needed three days in a cabin to grieve . . . or, feeling underappreciated, we wanted time with the uplifting person who's unofficial president of our personal fan club . . . or a child was feeling neglected, so we spent spring break on the shore, building sand castles, playing volleyball and flying kites, restoring family harmony and reviving some of the child suppressed in the busy parent . . . or a couple who talked only about bills and schedules grabbed the chance to spend uninterrupted time together, sleeping late and going for walks, chatting and rubbing each other's backs, having romantic dinners and making love.

Whatever it was for, that reservation number represents nothing in the gross national product; it was probably a loss to business and an affront to efficiency. After those vacation days, the messages had piled up on the answering machine, and the desk was thick with work undone. But in God's scheme, the time had incalculable merit. As Nicholas Evans writes in *The Horse Whisperer*:

> *She thought but didn't say, what a perilous commodity love was and that the proper calibration of its giving and taking was too precise by far for mere humans.*[2]

Such delicate calibration doesn't compute. It would drive accountants crazy; it wouldn't fit onto the ledgers. But it is the stuff of which love is made; a commodity too precious by far to erase from the calendar. If we didn't include it in the values we rank highest, we'd risk losing something intrinsic to ourselves, some glimmer of the way God sees us.

Any calendar worth its salt records a number of cross-outs, changed plans, last-minute additions and postponements. These aren't the long-planned events, but the compromises, delays, and impulses. In a larger sense, they may be the cracks where grace sneaks in.

Remember the seminar that got canceled? The free time that resulted seemed like a gift, coming at a time when we didn't even know how tired we were, how much we needed that breathing space.

Or the blizzard that unexpectedly wiped out two days of plans? It created a time at home by the fireplace to read a novel we'd put on hold, see a video we'd never had time for, have a conversation that turned out to be pivotal.

Filling in for a colleague at the last minute seemed initially like a burden, but became a rare, creative opportunity. Even an illness that put projects on hold gave us some slow days to savor what health means, to reflect on the miracle of "ordinary time," to envision what step was next, what larger directions we wanted to take. And that split-second decision to have dinner with Sonja? Ah—during that conversation we reached an important insight about ourselves, heard ourselves saying things we never expected. A couple hours' investment led to rich rewards.

THE PERSPECTIVE OF TIME

Looking back over a calendar with the perspective of a year or six months gives us a distance we didn't have as the days flew past. Just as we leaf through pictures in a photo album, watch old home videos, or look back from the pinnacle of a fiftieth birthday or twenty-fifth anniversary, we can sometimes savor more in retrospect than we did in the flash of the moment. When we are not totally caught up in the present, we may be more attuned to the subtle ways God is working over the long haul. What seemed like a crisis showed how well we could cope with the unexpected; what seemed like a disaster brought blessing in the long run. Something we treated casually at the time had important consequences several months later. If we try seriously to pray the texts of our lives, the calendar is a helpful prompt, an invaluable record.

When a loved one dies, people often say how glad they are they spent time with the person, or how sad they are for having missed the chance. It's a natural impulse when emotions run high. But when we reflect on a calendar, we don't need the harsh impetus of death to see that time with this person was well spent, or to resolve to spend more time with that person in the future. Doing the calendar reflection brings many people the dramatic realization that they are wasting inordinate amounts of time on people and projects they don't care much about, while shirking those they *say* they value most highly. Have we stumbled upon an exercise in values clarification here?

Perhaps, but it's also more. It is a realization of the saints among us, the abiding presence of God, the saving net of grace, the gifts of health, commitments, and work. If the calendar were totally blank, where could we say we'd invested our time and talent, where would we find a record of the blows and the joys? If we need any explanation of why we're tired, how we've responded or failed to respond to grace, the calendar provides it. It may show us why we feel fulfilled or why we feel unchallenged.

Even the most reflective exercise must stretch a bit to remember the things the calendar doesn't record. Perhaps these are better contained in other vessels: the journal, the memory, the heart. But across the weeks and months, a few moments sound like bells. A phone call, a word of encouragement, a glimpse of beauty—such small things sanctify our days.

Perhaps Alfred's prayer should be written on the calendar space for January 1 and consulted again on December 31 every year. It's a potent reminder that no matter how quickly the months pass, something abides. What may seem like unmotivated activity, wasted time, or frantic pursuit of obscure goals may in fact be God's carrying us, going before. What may seem like aimless wandering may in fact be purposeful journeying. In

God's design, it all makes sense. So should it in ours: God scripts the opening scene, each act, and the final curtain.

REFLECT

Have you ever thought of your calendar or Day-Timer as a prompt for prayer? What's helpful in the concept? What's not?

PRAY

(You saw this coming.) Choose a stretch of time on your calendar, perhaps six months or a year. Reflect back on it; look ahead. Where do you see God's fingerprints?

NOTES

CHAPTER 1
Many Faces: Toward a Broader Definition of Prayer

1. Richard Hauser, "Give Comfort to My People: Praying in the Spirit," *America,* 29 November 1997, 17.

2. Frank J. Houdek, S.J., *Guided by the Spirit: A Jesuit Perspective on Spiritual Direction* (Chicago: Loyola Press, 1996), 100–101.

3. *Catechism of the Catholic Church* (Chicago: Loyola University Press, 1994), 2558.

CHAPTER 2
Between the Hyacinth and the Laundry Pile:
Prayer as a Balancing Act

1. John Kavanaugh, *The Word Engaged* (Maryknoll, N.Y.: Orbis Books, 1997), 38–39.

2. Bill Huebsch, *A Radical Guide for Catholics: Rooted in the Essentials of Our Faith* (Mystic, Conn.: Twenty-Third Publications, 1992), 22.

CHAPTER 3
The Invisible Line, the Theseus Thread: Prayer That Anchors

1. George MacDonald, *The Princess and the Goblin* (New York: Macmillan, 1951), 120.

CHAPTER 4
Public Prayer: Warts and Blessings

1. Thomas Merton, *Conjectures of a Guilty Bystander* (Garden City, N.Y.: Doubleday, Image Books, 1968), 295.

2. Roger Mahony, "Gather Faithfully Together: A Guide for Sunday Mass," *Origins* 27, no. 15 (25 September 1997): 242–46.

3. John Shea, "Eucharist: Broken Bread Makes Us Whole," *U.S. Catholic,* February 1998, 14.

4. Anne Lamott, *Bird by Bird* (New York: Doubleday, 1994), 99.

5. Quoted in Mahony, 243.

CHAPTER 5
The Genuine Thing: Prayer That Honors Reality

1. Quoted in Martin Marty, *A Cry of Absence* (San Francisco: Harper and Row, 1983), 11.

2. Ibid., 7.

3. Ibid., 12.

4. Brett Hoover, *Losing Your Religion, Finding Your Faith* (Mahwah, N.J.: Paulist Press, 1998), 15.

5. Karl Rahner, quoted in Bill Huebsch, *A New Look at Prayer* (Mystic, Conn.: Twenty-Third Publications, 1992), 33.

6. Dorothy Day, quoted in Robert Coles, "On Moral Leadership: Dorothy Day and Peter Maurin in Tandem," *America*, 6 June 1998, 6–7.

7. Walter Brueggemann, *Finally Comes the Poet* (Minneapolis: Fortress Press, 1989), 3.

8. Nicholas Evans, *The Horse Whisperer* (New York: Dell, 1995), 322.

9. Daniel Berrigan, quoted in Megan McKenna, *Lent* (Maryknoll, N.Y.: Orbis Books, 1996), 221.

CHAPTER 6
The Soul's Native Land: The Context of Prayer

1. Murray Bodo and Susan Saint Sing, *A Retreat with Francis and Clare of Assisi* (Cincinnati: St. Anthony Messenger Press, 1996), vii–viii.

2. Thomas Merton, *Conjectures of a Guilty Bystander* (Garden City, N.Y.: Doubleday, Image Books, 1968), 257.

3. Ibid., 179.

4. Ed Ingebretsen, *Psalms of the Still Country* (San Jose, Calif.: Resource Publications, 1982), 95.

5. Ed Ingebretsen, *To Keep from Singing* (San Jose, Calif.: Resource Publications, 1985), 1.

6. Ingebretsen, *Psalms*, 96.

7. Psalms 121:1; 43:3; 125:2.

CHAPTER 7
The Trouble with Prayer: And Some Solutions

1. Quoted in Therese Borchard, ed., *Woman, Why Are You Weeping?* (New York: Crossroad, 1997), 24.

2. Ibid., 25.

3. Kathleen Norris, *The Cloister Walk* (New York: Riverhead Books, 1997), 366–67.

4. Etty Hillesum, *An Interrupted Life* (New York: Washington Square Press, 1985), 271.

5. Ibid., 267, 266, 260, 253, 258–59.

6. Ibid., 261.

7. Ibid., 263.

8. Ibid., 189.

9. Ibid., 247.

10. Ibid., 240.

CHAPTER 8
Prayer and Temperament:
Adapting Prayer Styles to Personality Types

1. David Keirsey and Marilyn Bates, *Please Understand Me* (Del Mar, Calif.: Prometheus Nemesis, 1984), 23.

2. LaVonne Neff, *One of a Kind* (Portland, Ore.: Multnomah, 1988), 155.

3. Roger O'Brien, "Four Ways to Become Holy," *U.S. Catholic*, March 1996, 21.

4. Chester Michael and Marie Norrisey, *Prayer and Temperament* (Charlottesville, Va.: Open Door, 1984).

CHAPTER 9
Ordinary Time: Praying the Texts of Our Lives

1. Joan Chittister, *Wisdom Distilled from the Daily* (New York: HarperCollins, 1991), 53–54.

2. Ibid., 58.

CHAPTER 10
Fluent in Many Tongues: The Languages of Prayer

1. Joseph Bernardin, *The Gift of Peace* (Chicago: Loyola Press, 1997), 67–68.

2. Quoted in Maggie Oman, ed., *Prayers for Healing* (Berkeley, Calif.: Conari Press, 1998), 7.

3. Thomas Merton, *Conjectures of a Guilty Bystander* (Garden City, N.Y.: Doubleday, Image Books, 1968), 178.

4. Leonore Fleischer, *Shadowlands* (London: Headline Book Publishing, 1994), 145.

CHAPTER 11
Sense Appeal: Metaphors for Prayer

1. Herman Melville, *Moby Dick* (New York: Library of America, 1983), 796.

2. Quoted in J. Robert Baker and others, eds., *A Baptism Sourcebook* (Chicago: Liturgy Training Publications, 1993), 101.

CHAPTER 12
Callused Hands: Working Prayer, Praying Work

1. Carol Perry, "The Noontime Prayer Revolution," *America*, 18 April 1998, 19.

2. Ibid.

3. Joan Chittister, *Wisdom Distilled from the Daily* (New York: HarperCollins, 1991), 90.

4. Thich Nhat Hanh, *Peace Is Every Step* (New York: Bantam, 1992), 80.

CHAPTER 13
Thank God! A Grateful Prayer

1. John McQuiston, *Always We Begin Again: The Benedictine Way of Living*. (Harrisburg, Pa.: Morehouse Publishing, 1996), 17–18.

2. Quoted in J. Robert Baker and others, eds., *A Baptism Sourcebook* (Chicago: Liturgy Training Publications, 1993), 90.

3. Henri Nouwen, *With Burning Hearts* (Maryknoll, N.Y.: Orbis Books, 1994), 93.

CHAPTER 14
Transforming Time: A Liturgy of the Hours

1. Catherine of Siena, "On Divine Providence," in *The Liturgy of the Hours*, vol. 2 (New York: Catholic Book Publishing, 1976), 1794.

2. Ibid., 1795.

CHAPTER 15
Journey to Jerusalem: The Prayer of Imagination

1. Diarmuid O'Murchu, *Quantum Theology* (New York: Crossroad, 1998), 120.

2. Anne Kelly, "To 'Reconstitute the World,'" in *The Candles Are Still Burning*, ed. Mary Grey and others (Collegeville, Minn: Liturgical Press, 1995), 13, 15, 16.

3. Walter Brueggemann, *Finally Comes the Poet* (Minneapolis: Fortress Press, 1989), 142.

4. Ibid., 7.

5. Jane Vennard, *Praying with Body and Soul* (Minneapolis: Augsburg Fortress, 1998), 75.

6. William Barry, S.J., *Finding God in All Things* (Notre Dame, Ind.: Ave Maria Press, 1991), 80.

7. Kelly, 19.

8. Ibid., 11.

9. Kathleen Norris, *The Cloister Walk* (New York: Riverhead Books, 1997), 338.

CHAPTER 16
Taming the Wolf: A Channel to Peace

1. Thich Nhat Hanh, *Peace Is Every Step* (New York: Bantam, 1992), 54.

2. Ibid., 53.

3. Joyce Denham, *A Child's Book of Celtic Prayers* (Chicago: Loyola Press, 1998), 13.

CHAPTER 17
Prayer in Paralysis: The Voice of Grief

1. Wallace Stegner, *Crossing to Safety* (New York: Penguin Books, 1987), 274–75.

2. Ibid., 275.

3. Henri Nouwen, *With Burning Hearts* (Maryknoll, N.Y.: Orbis Books, 1994), 40.

4. Ibid., 73

5. Martin Marty, *A Cry of Absence* (San Francisco: Harper and Row, 1983), 136, 139.

6. Robin Behn, "Paper Bird," quoted in J. Robert Baker and others, eds., *A Baptism Sourcebook* (Chicago: Liturgy Training Publications, 1993), 51.

7. Diarmuid O'Murchu, *Quantum Theology* (New York: Crossroad, 1998), 35.

8. Elizabeth Jennings, *Collected Poems*, quoted in *A Baptism Sourcebook*, 80.

CHAPTER 18
The Saints: A Conversation among Friends

1. Quoted in Gail Ramshaw, *Words around the Table* (Chicago: Liturgy Training Publications, 1991), 54.

2. Robert Ellsberg, *All Saints* (New York: Crossroad, 1998), 476.

3. Thomas Merton, *The Seven Storey Mountain* (New York: Harcourt Brace, 1948), 238.

4. Monica Furlong, *Merton: A Biography* (San Francisco: Harper and Row, 1980), 237.

5. Carol Lee Flinders, *Enduring Grace* (New York: HarperSanFrancisco, 1993), 38–39.

6. Ibid., 39.

7. Murray Bodo and Susan Saint Sing, *A Retreat with Francis and Clare of Assisi* (Cincinnati: St. Anthony Messenger Press, 1996), 32.

8. Furlong, 283.

9. Catherine de Hueck Doherty, *Poustinia* (Fount Paperbacks, 1975), 92.

10. Ibid., 270.

11. Flinders, 185.

12. Ellsberg, 30.

13. Flinders, 124.

14. Ibid., 115.

15. Carol Lee Flinders, *At the Root of This Longing* (New York: HarperSanFrancisco, 1998), 3–4.

CHAPTER 19
In Closing: A Calendar

1. Bill Huebsch, "The Church in the Modern World," in *Vatican II in Plain English: The Constitutions* (Allen, Tex.: Thomas More, 1997), 158.

2. Nicholas Evans, *The Horse Whisperer* (New York: Dell, 1995), 296.

BIBLIOGRAPHY

Baker, J. Robert, and others, eds. *A Baptism Sourcebook*. Chicago: Liturgy Training
     Publications, 1993.

Bernardin, Joseph. *The Gift of Peace*. Chicago: Loyola Press, 1997.

Bodo, Murray, and Susan Saint Sing. *A Retreat with Francis and Clare of Assisi*.
     Cincinnati: St. Anthony Messenger Press, 1996.

Boland, Eavan. *An Origin Like Water*. New York: W. W. Norton, 1996.

Borchard, Therese, ed. *Woman, Why Are You Weeping?* New York: Crossroad, 1997.

Brueggemann, Walter. *Finally Comes the Poet*. Minneapolis: Fortress Press, 1989.

Chittister, Joan. *Wisdom Distilled from the Daily*. New York: HarperCollins, 1991.

Coles, Robert. "On Moral Leadership: Dorothy Day and Peter Maurin in Tandem."
     America, 6 June 1998, 6–9.

Denham, Joyce. *A Child's Book of Celtic Prayers*. Chicago: Loyola Press, 1998.

Dillard, Annie. *Teaching a Stone to Talk*. New York: Harper and Row, 1982.

Ellsberg, Robert. *All Saints*. New York: Crossroad, 1998.

Evans, Nicholas. *The Horse Whisperer*. New York: Dell, 1995.

Fleischer, Leonore. *Shadowlands*. London: Headline Book Publishing, 1994.

Flinders, Carol Lee. *At the Root of This Longing*. New York: Harper SanFrancisco, 1998.

———. *Enduring Grace*. New York: Harper SanFrancisco, 1993.

Furlong, Monica. *Merton: A Biography*. San Francisco: Harper and Row, 1980.

Graham, Gerry. "To Attain the Love of Beauty." In *Studies in the Spirituality of Jesuits* (May 1998).

Grey, Mary, and others, eds. *The Candles Are Still Burning*. Collegeville, Minn.: Liturgical Press, 1995.

Hauser, Richard. "Give Comfort to My People: Praying in the Spirit." *America*, 29 November 1997, 17–18.

Hillesum, Etty. *An Interrupted Life*. New York: Washington Square Press, 1985.

Hoover, Brett. *Losing Your Religion, Finding Your Faith*. Mahweh, N.J.: Paulist Press, 1998.

Houdek, Frank J. *Guided by the Spirit: A Jesuit Perspective on Spiritual Direction*. Chicago: Loyola Press, 1996.

Huebsch, Bill. *A New Look at Prayer: Searching for Bliss*. Mystic, Conn.: Twenty-Third Publications, 1992.

———. *A Radical Guide for Catholics: Rooted in the Essentials of Our Faith*. Mystic, Conn.: Twenty-Third Publications, 1992.

———. *Vatican II in Plain English: The Constitutions*. Allen, Tex.: Thomas More, 1997.

Ingebretsen, Ed. *Psalms of the Still Country*. San Jose, Calif.: Resource Publications, 1982.

————. *To Keep from Singing*. San Jose, Calif.: Resource Publications, 1985.

Kavanaugh, John. *The Word Engaged*. Maryknoll, N.Y.: Orbis Books, 1997.

Lamott, Anne. *Bird by Bird*. New York: Doubleday, 1994.

The Liturgy of the Hours. New York: Catholic Book Publishing, 1976.

MacDonald, George. *The Princess and the Goblin*. New York: Macmillan, 1951.

Mahony, Roger. "Gather Faithfully Together: A Guide for Sunday Mass." *Origins*. vol. 27, no. 15 (25 September 1977): 242–46.

Marty, Martin. *A Cry of Absence*. San Francisco: Harper and Row, 1983.

McQuiston, John. *Always We Begin Again: The Benedictine Way of Living*. Harrisburg, Pa.: Morehouse Publishing, 1996.

Melville, Herman. *Moby Dick*. New York: Library of America, 1983.

Merton, Thomas. *Conjectures of a Guilty Bystander*. Garden City, N.Y.: Doubleday, Image Books, 1968

————. *The Seven Storey Mountain*. New York: Harcourt Brace, 1948.

Michael, Chester, and Marie Norrisey. *Prayer and Temperament*. Charlottesville, Va.: Open Door, 1984.

Neff, LaVonne. *One of a Kind*. Portland, Ore.: Multnomah, 1988.

Nhat Hanh, Thich. *Peace Is Every Step*. New York: Bantam, 1992.

Norris, Kathleen. *The Cloister Walk*. New York: Riverhead Books, 1997.

Nouwen, Henri. *With Burning Hearts*. Maryknoll, N.Y.: Orbis Books, 1994.

O'Brien, Roger. "Four Ways to Become Holy." *U.S. Catholic*, March 1996, 17–23.

O'Murchu, Diarmuid. *Quantum Theology*. New York: Crossroad, 1998.

Pennington, M. Basil. *I Call You Friends*. St. Louis, Mo.: Creative Communications for the Parish, 1996.

Perry, Carol. "The Noontime Prayer Revolution." *America*, 18 April 1998, 18–20.

Ramshaw, Gail. *Words around the Table*. Chicago: Liturgy Training Publications, 1991.

Roberts, Elizabeth, and Elias Amidon, eds. *Earth Prayers*. New York: HarperSan Francisco, 1991.

Rupp, Joyce. *Dear Heart, Come Home*. New York: Crossroad, 1996.

Schreck, Nancy, and Maureen Leach. *Psalms Anew*. Winona, Minn.: St. Mary's Press, 1986.

Shea, John. "Eucharist: Broken Bread Makes Us Whole." *U.S. Catholic*, February 1998, 10–16.

Stegner, Wallace. *Crossing to Safety*. New York: Penguin Books, 1987.

Vennard, Jane. *Praying with Body and Soul*. Minneapolis: Augsburg Fortress, 1998.